Blue Lines

by Thomas Reed

Cornmill
PRESS

Blue Lines
© 2010, 2022 Thomas Reed

Printed in the United States of America

ISBN 978-1-7333422-2-3

1 2 3 4 5 6 7 8 9 10

Cover and internal design by James Daley

Cornmill Press
16420 SE 31st Street
Bellevue, WA 98008
1-509-828-3300
cornmillpress.com

For Dad, who got it all started

Contents

Blue Lines and Blue-Lining

My fishing pal and colleague Chris Hunt is a big guy. He's the kind of guy who might have played offensive tackle for the old WAC back in the day if he had wanted to. But Chris instead went to Colorado's Western State—or "Wasted State" as it is known in some circles—to fly fish and drink beer.

Western is in the heart of the southern Rockies and it is in the heart of Colorado's best fishing. Just west of town, the spirit of the famed Gunnison River and its willow flies lies buried beneath Blue Mesa Reservoir. Chris and I were yet to be born when the river was drowned, but when I was the editor of Gunnison's newspaper many years later, the old timers were still carrying the death of the river on their shoulders. Fishing men like Mac McGraw mourned the river daily and talked of the days of famous anglers like Ernest Schwiebert. Mac snorted that Blue Mesa was the "world's biggest sucker hole" and he wrote remembrances of the mountain river that made one wish you were born a generation earlier just to have seen it. It was a river of big trout and big bugs and bamboo.

Chris ended up at Western because he likes to fish. In one of life's crazy near-misses, I did my tour there just a few years earlier, writing outdoor columns and covering city council meetings, hunting the surrounding hills for elk and deer, and slogging my way into far-back country in search of little trout on small streams. I was lucky enough to work for a Texas oilman who owned the paper and also owned miles of the best trout stream around—the Taylor. I got to fish it just before a famous fisherman named Jimmy Carter came to visit and fish the same stretch of crystal water dancing between black boulders and harboring brown and rainbow trout as long as a man's thigh.

A year or so after I left for another job in another town near trout, Chris came along and worked for the same paper, doing the same job I'd left. It wasn't until years later that we met each other and discovered we'd followed the same paths in career, and the same dim trails into high country streams.

We did not discover our near-intersection until one day in the Wyoming Range when we were thrashing through thick willows on a tributary of the Greys River. The Greys is one of the West's most beautiful and accessible trout streams. Its entire course is on public land, more than fifty miles of fishable water. It cleaves the Wyoming Range and the Salt River Range through some of the prettiest standing-on-end country I've ever seen. And, it is home to pure Snake River cutthroat trout. Its tributaries are too.

This time, I was following Chris instead of the other way around, quite literally. It's always a good idea to follow a bigger person through thick brush and Chris was clearing out a moose-sized tunnel that I could make my way through. I just kept a distance so I wouldn't get whipped in the face by errant branches.

We burst out onto the banks of the little stream on a gravel bar that led into a beautiful riffle where the crick bent beneath willow trunks and around algae-slicked boulders. I gave Chris the first cast. After all, he had just done all of the hard work. So he crawled up to the stream, made one back-cast and put his fly on the water. It bobbed along for a second and then there was a swirl and a fish was on. A fifteen-inch Snake River cutthroat.

Without even taking the fish out of the water, Chris twisted the fly out of its mouth, cast again a little higher into the pool, and caught the twin brother. And again. Triplets. I stood back waiting until it was my turn.

Chris turned to me, wiped his hand on his shirt and then wiped the sweat out of his eyes and smiled.

"I love blue-lining."

"Blue-lining?" I asked.

"You know, fishing those blue lines on the map, those thin blue lines."

Chris, like me, is a small-stream guy, a guy who would rather be on a creek somewhere in the forest, far away from trails and people, than on the glorious Madison in a drift boat surrounded by rising brown trout. When he gets to new country, he pulls out a Forest Service map and finds those lines of blue. They start in tall far-back country and cascade through canyon and chasm. A few have trails, but if you walk far enough from your vehicle, if you push into the depths and move those muscles, you will put people behind you and find trout ahead. Then there are the blue lines that have no trails—where a fisherman bent upon catching must stumble and slip through thick timber, or scramble down rough canyons, or thrash like a wallowed Hereford through patches of willow. Blue lines. Lots of fish. Sometimes broken rods. Not from the fish, but from working a delicate piece of graphite through thick brush with an off-balance way of going. It's a country that is tough on fly rods and tougher on tendons.

It occurred to me that day on the banks of the blue line that fed the Greys that feeds the Snake that feeds the Columbia, that I had been blue lining all of my life. I just never had a name for it.

I don't ever remember not fishing. I don't remember why I even started or why I became so addicted. I practiced fly-casting out on the front lawn before I was a teenager. I read all the magazines and followed the instructions and got a passable cast. I dug earthworms out of thick soil and threaded them wiggling and bleeding worm blood onto a hook and I caught brook trout in mountain streams. I trolled strange lures called Flatfish, painted yellow with red spots, in a small aluminum boat on a western Colorado lake with my brother, my dad and Dad's best friend from high school in Estes Park. I fished high lakes and I followed blue lines. Sometimes the blue lines led to blue dots—high mountain lakes—and sometimes the blue lines were not razor thin, but thick rivers. But mostly, my fishing was small stream, born of snowmelt and mountain spring. Up high. Up where there weren't any other people for miles around. Blue lines.

Not long ago, Chris and I were standing on the banks of another Wyoming Range trout stream with Frank Smethurst, the host of *Trout on the Rise*, a television program of the nonprofit group Trout Unlimited. Frank is a southpaw who throws one of the tightest and prettiest loops I've ever seen a fly caster toss. He made himself somewhat famous in fly-fishing circles by producing a hilarious short film called *Running Down the Man* about fly-fishing for rooster fish off the coast of Baja. It is a frantic, fast-paced film that follows Frank in chaotic wind sprints up and down the beach as he tries to get out ahead of surf-cruising rooster fish. Now he's covering the states for Trout Unlimited. In the Wyoming Range, he was out to catch the Cutt-Slam, which is a program of the Wyoming Game and Fish Department that recognizes fishermen for catching each of the four native cutthroat trout in their home waters. *Trout on the Rise* was covering Frank's quest to do so.

On this little tributary of the Green River we were talking about Colorado River cutthroat trout subspecies and why gas drilling rigs should not be put right on the banks of trout streams—actually we were standing on an old drill pad that was a stone's throw from the water's edge and looking down at this small stream that carried a significant silt load from the recent industrial activities—when it happened.

It being wind.

You don't really experience wind until you experience Wyoming wind. After living for years in Wyoming and casting a fly line in Wyoming wind, every cast I ever made in all kinds of wind everywhere else was easy. Today's wind was a doozie. It came off the high peaks of the range and it slammed us right in the face. Frank had yet to catch his Colorado River cutt, so he and the camera crew scrambled down the bank and went at it, despite the wind. I looked at Hunt.

"Let's go sit in the truck and drink coffee."

For an hour, Frank stood in that wind, casting a four-weight rod. This was the kind of wind that takes your fly line and throws it back into your face. But Frank stood there. He caught a lot of brook trout. He made a lot of casts. Almost all of them hit the water, despite the wind that would have put a lesser caster into deep despair. Finally, after a long time of standing out in the cold wind of that late August day, he caught and landed an eight-inch Colorado Cutthroat trout. Blue-lining. Literally, but figuratively as well. Frank was enduring. So was the crew, two with heavy cameras and one taking care of the sound, trying to shield as much wind as possible. Blue-lining. All of them.

I've started to think of blue-lining more as a metaphor for all kinds of fishing. The tough kind. The type of fishing that isn't easy, that causes you to sweat and curse and prevail. The kind of fishing where no one other than you mans the oars or ties on your flies or hunkers down in a hail storm that throws marbles out of the sky. It's attitude more than action, blue-lining. You can blue-line your way into a flung-back mountain lake, or a fish-less day on a big famous river can call for a blue-lining attitude.

Indeed, it's more a paradigm for life. It's not easy. There will be tough days—maybe even years—and thin reward. But once in a while, if you prevail, if you pick yourself up, climb one more scree and talus slope to another pool up ahead, you will find reward for your hard work.

The worst boss I ever had gave me the best piece of advice: "If it were easy," he said, "anybody could do it."

That is blue-lining.

Big rivers speak of adventure, of mysteries in deep holes and around shadowed bends. They talk to you of downward flows, of going places guided by gravity and water. They entice you into their currents. You want to go, to launch a drift boat into whispering water, and to float away around and down those curves.

Small streams, on the other hand, call you home, call you to the heart, to the source. I have seldom been on a small stream without wanting to climb upstream to its source, to see the ground in high country where the stream is born. Perhaps this place is a spring shaded by purple monkeyflower. Perhaps the stream is the offspring of several parents—multiple branches draining big country. But even more than calling me to climb into the high country, small streams call me back to my roots, to a time when I carried a worm-baited hook instead of a fly rod, to a time when a trophy fish was an eight-inch-long brook trout that was cooked on a stick over a campfire and eaten with a sprinkling of salt and pepper.

In the end, given a choice, I will take the small stream. I will take the small stream for its cold and clear current, for the way it challenges and shapes the land, for the way it bends and drops and pools. I will take the small stream for the grizzly bear and cougar tracks that line its banks, for the elk and moose scat that sprinkles its shoulders, for the gravel bars clean of bootprints. But more than anything, I will take the small stream over the river for its trout. They generally won't be as large, nor as sophisticated, but they will be a heck of a lot of fun to catch.

If you like to catch fish and a lot of fish, a small stream is a good place to start. On our Western rivers, many of the trout have been hyper-educated by the drift of many a fly. But on a small stream, especially one that has been climbed to and scrambled alongside, you will do well with just a little skill.

A stream, in my thinking, is any water that is too small for navigation, even in the smallest of kayaks or canoes. A small stream, too, has a personality. It has fast water and slow, but each of these stretches is short enough to not be boring, and full of enough structure to have character. There's a small stream in southeastern Wyoming I know that has lots of flat water, but the thing snakes and loops back on itself so much that, if you pulled it out straight, it would reach from Nebraska to Utah. It is the curves that give it character, the big bends with deep undercut banks, the current lines and willow runs. You can spend a day here and feel like you are getting to know it a little bit. A day on a big river can be less friendly, and your depth of knowledge is only as long as that day. The next day could be completely different.

The key to fishing a small stream, more than equipment or files, or technique, is water reading. In small streams, pools are the key. Sometimes the pools can be the result of structure in the stream—a log or boulder—but sometimes the pool is formed by a bend in the stream, by the stream meeting a bank, then turning back upon itself. In all pools, there are lines and these lines show you where to cast.

Imagine a stream completely devoid of structure except one big boulder. The stream bends around the boulder and the current forms two visible lines in the water, one to the left, the other to the right. Casting from downstream, a fly placed on either of these lines will drift to trout. Current lines are often where trout hold, riding the flow, waiting for food to be swept from the faster water into the slow. This is usually at the head of the pool.

The body of the pool is that water behind the boulder that is flat water, pooling gracefully, before tailing out into the current again. This, too, is a good place for a trout to hold. In small pools, the blend between the head of a pool and the body of a pool is blurred and you will do well to cast to both.

In the tail of a pool, fish will hold where the current starts to pick up again, sweeping off the bottom of the pool and into faster water before carrying on downstream. If you are fishing upstream, climbing the stream towards its source, then this is where you want to make your initial casts, catching the fish that are held in the tail before trying to cast into the body. The reason, of course, is that you don't want to cast over fish when you should be catching them.

Stream bends have the same phenomena as structure in the stream, but the line is a single one formed by the current. Many times, the bend itself forms a pool, as the current sweeps one direction, then curls back upon itself. In big water, I've seen fish face downstream where they took food drifting on the upstream eddy.

But in small streams, usually the eddy is too small for this kind of behavior. Instead, fish use the eddy line and the pool formed by the eddy as hiding cover and feeding zones. Casting into the tail end of the eddy pool, and then working up the line formed by the slower water and fast, will be hitting places where trout like to hold.

Observation plays an important role in fishing a small stream. Take a moment now and then to sit on a stream side rock, smoke a good cigar and just watch. One of my favorite outdoor writers was Ted Trueblood. I'd read his articles by flashlight late at night growing up, way past my bedtime. Ted often wrote of sitting down and smoking a pipe when he got into a place where there was game or fish. It's a good image. Instead of rushing at it, fish-crazed and wild-eyed without a plan, sit down and smoke a pipe. Slow down and observe the way. You'll be rewarded by good observations of wildlife and bird life, but you'll also be honing your fishing expertise.

Once on a small stream in Wyoming's Bighorn Mountains, I was drawing a complete blank with a hopper pattern. I couldn't figure out why because there were hoppers along the stream, and good numbers of them. But then I realized something: it wasn't windy, which for Wyoming, caught me off-guard. The fact that it was dead calm had been nagging at me all day long. I couldn't figure out what was going on until it dawned upon me that there wasn't even the slightest puff of a breeze and the hoppers simply weren't getting blown into the water. As I sat there, I started looking not at the more obvious terrestrials like hoppers, but at the aquatic insects. I then realized that there was the standard hatch of brown caddis coming off the water. I switched to a caddis nymph, added a strike indicator, and started catching fish.

For equipment, I like to go light. Usually this means a four-weight rod. I have a great four-weight that my brother gave me one Christmas. I have it loaded with weight-forward floating line and in even the stiffest wind, it casts pretty. It's got enough spine for a bigger streamer, but usually I keep it rigged with smaller flies, particularly dries and small nymphs. I have fished with smaller rods, on down to a two-weight, or even an aught. The four is a better choice, at least in Western wind that can make casting difficult. I want my fly rod to be fast enough and have enough punch to get through it. I also like the fact that even though my four-weight is eight-and-a-half feet long, it isn't so long as to interfere with streamside foliage. Generally, as you drop in weight, you also lose length, and I like a bit longer fly rod that lets me get a little longer cast.

In a small stream, you shouldn't have to worry too much about backing for your fly line and a huge selection of flies. I have heard that double-taper line allows you to place a little more delicate cast than weight-forward line because the front taper is generally longer than in a weight-forward line. I haven't tried that myself, but I recently bought another spool for my reel to test that theory.

There are three kinds of techniques that I like to use when fishing small streams. The first is the standard dead drift technique of nymph fishing, essentially casting into current and watching your fly line for the slightest hesitation. The second is the standard dry fly drift, casting to the edge of current where your fly can bounce, but not drown. The last, and one of the most fun, is the skitter technique.

This technique calls for casting downstream, and holding all of the line and leader off the water, creating a somewhat life-like "skitter" that would imitate an adult mayfly dapping across the surface of the water. It's a fun technique, but you'll have to calm your nerves and let the trout take the fly because this is the easiest way to yank the fly out of the trout's mouth. Sometimes you can even see the fish coming as it shoots toward the fly and you really have to work on not jerking the fly away.

I think line control is important. Some people think you don't have to mend line in small streams, but I find myself doing mini-mends, just little flips of line to get a good drift. This is especially important in faster water when the length of a drift may be only a few feet, or in some cases, a few inches.

Finally, probably the best thing about small streams is that you can fish them without your whole arsenal of flies. A good nymph pattern, perhaps a good small streamer pattern, and two dry patterns is all you'll need. You don't have to go crazy with fly sizes either—shoot for sizes twelve to sixteen and you'll be all set. I like a caddis imitation that can be tied a little larger to imitate a hopper, perhaps a mayfly imitation, and a bunch of nymphs in colors from dark brown to black. That's it. Sure, you may be out of luck when there's a hatch of flying ants or something, but in most cases, small stream trout aren't as selective as their river cousins and will take most anything.

After a day of doing this, following a small stream up into the country, you'll feel like you've gotten to know something about the place. Then, when you go back the next time, it will feel as if you are going to a familiar, comfortable place called home.

And so. *Blue Lines.* The names have mostly been changed to protect the innocent. We who fish—or hunt—are a verbose lot. We sit at bars and lean our elbows on slick wood sticky with old beer and we talk about the things we have seen, the trout we have caught, the places we've been. While our tales may be embellished with glory and strife, they will mostly be true. But the names will be changed. No fisherman in his right mind reveals his secrets. They are personal, private, protected and the names are likely fabricated.

Trout Therapy

The big rivers do it to me. Spirit-crushers. All winter long, they beckon, so I go. But often I leave hurt, disappointed, positive that I really don't know how to fly fish after all.

I retreat to the mountains, battered and bruised. I repair. Swimming in the tiny headwaters are confidence feeders—therapy fish. Ego trout.

I belly crawl to the streams. Carefully, thoughtfully, I rise to my knees behind the willows and gently dap a small fly of any variety on the water. In a rush, a trout slams the fly and I set the hook.

But the hook-set is too much. My mind is in the mountains, but my arm and wrist are still on the big water. The trout shoots like a finned rocket over my head, suddenly wrenched from his water home into the cold mountain air. He dances on the hook, all of four inches, but hey, a fish nonetheless. I unpin him and drop him gently back into the stream. I cast again. Another fish. Again. Another.

The pattern is repeated. Gradually, my confidence grows. The trout are the shrinks and the stream is my couch.

Ego trout don't have to be of a single variety. My bloodied self-image has been boosted by browns and rainbows, cutts and goldens. But the king of the aquatic Freuds is the brookie.

You have to admire the brook trout. Biggest one I ever caught was about nineteen inches. And that one was a monster. I've never caught one even close to that size since. If I land a foot-long brook trout, I think I'm in heaven. Most are eight inches and less. Many are the size of those canned fish that they cover with mustard. But they do me well.

Brookies don't know how small they really are. They are quick to strike a fly, just as a terrier is quick to rush the back fence, barking fiercely at nothing at all. Most people get a little tired of terriers, just like most anglers shun brookies. I don't. I like brookies, especially after big river browns and rainbows have kicked me around a little and I'm in need of some couch time.

If you really want to look like you know what you are doing, take a friend who has never been fishing before. Don't bother explaining that the most important thing, the only crucial technique, is the ability to quietly sneak within casting range without scaring the little guys to death. Arrange a meeting time and go separate ways. When you reunite, compare notes. You will dazzle your companion with tales of twenty, thirty, even forty fish caught on your stealth attack. If your companion doesn't know the technique, there won't be many stories from the other party. A nasty trick, true, but darn good for the ego.

We give a lot of credit to brown trout and rightfully so. By the time a brown has graduated from the foot-long school, he has a Ph.D. tucked under one fin. Cast for him on any big Western river and you're matching wits with the best, even though his brain is about the size of the tip of your little finger. All your technique is brought to bear here. You carefully match the hatch. You measure the exact amount of leader, selecting just the right tippet. You cast straight and perfect. You mend line and keep a constant alert for the slightest movement that might indicate a strike. You have entered a contest—and one that you don't often win.

This is the river brown. But the crick (that's crick, not creek) brown is something entirely different. The crick brown is also an ego trout, a budding psychiatrist wanting to help you out. He swims deep in the clear pools of the little streams, ready to rise to a dry, eager to swoop in on a nymph. With stealth at the stream bank, you can sneak-fish up on him and land him. Aha! See, I can catch a brown trout after all.

Once on a small crick not far from where I live, I spent the day stalking ego browns. There were two challenges that day. The first was sneak-fishing up on my quarry. The second was dodging rattlesnakes in the sagebrush. But that's part of your ego recovery. Call it shock therapy.

Sure, I like catching those hell-bent, rod-breaking browns, those air-busting rainbows, those lunker high-mountain goldens. But on a late summer day after the rivers have chewed me up and spat me out, give me an ego fish. Or ten.

Then I'll be ready to take on the rivers again.

Where It Is Born

The Willys smells of thick grease and dust. It whines at top speed and rattles and we are going fishing. The early morning sun is just coming off the granite onto the ponderosas and Dad and Parker are laughing about something. They've known each other forever and they call each other by their last names as old high school football teammates do, even though they are well up into their forties now. Grown men with the high school years incredulously decades distant. How did that happen?

Char and I are in the back seat, swaying back and forth to the movement of the Jeep and I can feel my heart up and hammering in my chest. For the dozenth time, I ask how much farther and for the dozenth time I am told to hang on, not long now. And they turn back to laughing and telling private inside jokes and remembering.

We are headed to Bull Creek on an old dude ranch at the edge of Rocky Mountain National Park. The dude ranch has gone under, but Parker has an in with the new owner and we are going to fish on the ranch, and then up into the park. Pavement becomes washboard gravel becomes twin tracks with thick grass in the middle and we pass under the sign to the ranch, and Dad climbs out to get the gate and the Jeep grinds forward. There, before us, are the ranch buildings and horses standing three-legged lazy in July sun. Dad gets in again, we drive into the ranch yard and the adults get out, leaving me and my brother in the back. I think I'm going to pee myself I'm so excited. They stand around for a while, a long time it seems, talking, hands back-pocketed, spitting in the soil, laughing, kicking at hapless ants. Then Parker and Dad come back and Parker leans in and looks right at me and grins that grin that takes his eyes away into wrinkles and he laughs. "Okay, we're all set."

We take a spur road off the ranch road and tall grass brushes the underbelly of the Willys and we bounce for a while, following the stream, willows scraping against the Jeep and then we find a nice place under the outstretched branches of a ponderosa and now it's on. Dad hands me a fly rod, a steel rod that I can pull on and extend. A telescoping steel rod. There's a reel too, a reel that has a button you can push that zings in the fly line in a sudden, haywire snap. Dad and Parker show my brother and me how to string up the rods, and show us, again, the clinch knot. I dig around in my band-aid box packed with soil and find a worm squiggling red and slimy and I pull it out and wipe the crumbs of black dirt off of it and pin it and loop it onto the hook. It squirms around and dances there on the hook. We walk to the water and Parker cautions me about staying low.

"Watch what happens if you don't." And he stands.

I can see them, zipping left and right, and back and forth across the stream and then the pool is empty. There are no fish at all. "Okay, you got it?"

At my nod: "Let's sneak up to the next pool."

They take turns, the grown-ups, showing Char and me how to

cast, how to avoid snagging your line in the trees. They show us, but it doesn't work and I spend a lot of time taking the line out of the trees. Little trout spook again when I stand and shake tree branches and we move on up to the next pool.

It is a nice one, long and clear and cold and this time, I'm on my knees behind a big willow and I drop my line down into the water and feel the trout. I pull on the hook and a little fish is there, dancing on the end of my line. "That's a brookie," says Dad.

I'm grinning.

It goes like this, crawling and dropping worms over into the water. I dig around in my band-aid box for more worms and I try to tie my own hooks on. I start to get it. All of it. I'm catching now and Parker shows me how to knock the trout on the head, and how to slit it around the throat and up the belly and how stick your finger down past the sharp little teeth below the lower jaw and give the whole works a pull until the guts come out with a meaty tearing sound and how to thumb the bloodline off of the backbone and rinse the trout in the stream. Rinse your knife too. Gotta keep your knife clean. I've gone through all of my worms now and we almost have a limit of fish, all strung up on a willow switch that Char and I take turns carrying, like some glorious trophy from the battlefield. A garter snake darts in the grass and I see it and pounce on it and it pisses down my arm, but I don't care. "Can I keep it Dad?"

"Where are you going to put it?"

I dump out all of the dirt from the band-aid can. "In here?"

"Okay. Sure." He laughs.

Can I go up ahead on my own?

Dad laughs again and lights his pipe. "Sure."

There's a beaver pond up ahead, a stretch of flat water on the little stream, overhung with aspens and willows and a ponderosa a little farther back from the edge. I have no more worms though and the one left on the end of my hook has dried into a desiccated carcass. "Want to try a fly instead of a worm?"

"Okay."

Parker digs a wet fly out of an old cigar tin he keeps in his left shirt pocket and hands it to me. It's brown and made of feathers and fur and I look up at him. He grins. His eyes disappear again.

"Tie it on."

It takes me a while, but I do.

"Give it a whirl. Remember to stay low."

The pond is shaded by willow and it is not very large. It is more side channel than pond and I carefully crawl to the edge of the water, avoiding beaver-bitten sharp sticks that poke out of the grass like Viet Nam punji stakes, and look down into the depth. I see no fish. I do see the mouth of an underwater tunnel though, a place where the beaver move between food caches. I lean carefully out over the water and drop in the fly. It sinks and I watch it, clear and slowly sinking, down into the mouth of the tunnel, down deeper until it is nearly out of sight. Then, just as I lose sight of it, I see a fish dart from inside the tunnel, out into the light. It grabs my fly and I set the hook and the fish darts and dances on the line and I pull it up quickly and it is in the air and dancing in the air on my fly and I laugh. Laugh.

"Hey, Dad, Dad, I caught another one!"

The Day I Was Trendy

I think it happened in late July 1980.

Carl drove. We were high school buddies, pals who grew up together breathing the scent of rain on sagebrush and living for things like elk and trout and Western skies.

We had beer in a cooler and a couple of good cigars between us. Our fly rods were stashed in the back and we were headed out to fish the South Platte for a day. I may have even been wearing Carhartt pants.

I didn't know it then, but I know it now. At that exact moment, I was at the crest, at the peak, the pinnacle. I was cutting edge.

The vehicle we rode in was a 1969 Ford Bronco, the original sport utility vehicle, a four-wheel-drive invented before the term SUV. A true utility vehicle made for use in the rough country. No frills and who cares about the spills? At that very moment, Carl and I were pioneers: we had the SUV, we had the cigars, the beer, the clothing, the fly fishing gear.

Today, of course, the trend wave has passed me by. But for a moment there we were it.

I'm still fly fishing, but not the South Platte any more. In 1980, the river was famous, but not overrun. Plus the last time I was there, I definitely felt underdressed with my patched up waders, ten-year-old fly rod and ratty vest. Unless one has a brand new outfit with all the geegaws, a fancy new rod made of the latest graphite composite and wrap-around polarized sunglasses, one should stay away from such rivers.

Then there's the outfits in the parking lots. Carl's old Ford was what a four-wheel-drive should be. You could hear the highway humming away beneath your tires and you had to shift the thing with a lever on the steering column. It had two speeds: crawling and shouting. Crawling was for the big boulders you eased over on your way up some so-called jeep trail, heading to a small stream up high where you could smell the cool summer snow above timberline in the downstream wind. Shouting was a highway speed; you had to shout to make yourself heard over the whistling wind, humming tires and growling engine. Today's four-wheel-drives are more like luxury cars...at luxury car prices. There's power-everything, tilt-everything and should you—heaven forbid—spill a cup of coffee on the carpeting, you'll have to find yourself another fishing partner. Plus, after decades of investing in a retirement account, I finally have close to enough money to actually buy one.

Cigars, well, everyone and his mother smokes a cigar nowadays. There's a cigar shop in most upscale mountain trout towns and a whole slew of cigar etiquette, just like there's a wrong way and a right way to taste wine. For years, I have been lighting stogies, but I ran across something last month—a day by day cigar calendar, no less— that told me I had been doing it all wrong. Now I'm not even sure I know how to light the darn things. And you don't want to light them in your plush new four-by-four.

Then there's beer. You used to be able to quaff down whatever kind of beer you could get your hands on and feel pretty good about it. It didn't matter as long as it came in some kind of container and tasted good. Today, my friends turn their noses up at my beverage of choice. They prefer the new micro-brews made with ancient (five years old) recipes in funky little mountain towns all over the West. Stout, amber, bock, lager…the choices boggle your mind. Then there's your choice of flavorings: wheat, oatmeal, chili pepper, and…fruit juice, for crying out loud. Whatever happened to the two different kinds of beer I used to drink: cold and starting to get warm?

Finally, there's the clothing. I used to wear jeans jackets. I still wear Carhartt pants, but so does everybody else. I may even be wearing the same pair I was wearing back on that fateful day in 1980.

Don't get me wrong. There have been many improvements in my quality of life since 1980. I enjoy a good micro-brew and the economies that micro-breweries have spurred into towns that were dying back in 1980. I like a nice cigar grown somewhere other than a Mini Mart. I'm dying to get my hands on the latest introduction from Orvis and I've ridden (careful not to spill my coffee) in a big fancy shiny new four-by-four.

But every once in a while, I pine for that day in 1980 when Carl and I were tooling along enjoying the good life and not even knowing that we were leading the pack instead of following behind with our tongues hanging out.

The Endless Thirst of Grass

The sun never quits. It beats down on my shoulders, tans my arms and face a brown they've never been, fades and flakes the hide on the old pickup that they gave me to drive. At lunch, every lunch, I sit in the shade under the same cottonwood and eat apples and cheese. It is hot even here where it is supposed to be comfortable and I look off toward Flattop where the lodgepole pines are dark blue against the skyline. A cool blue.

Sometimes the badger that lives across the ditch is there and I smell him coming. It's a musky, skunky smell. First time he visited, I was sitting stretch-legged dreaming whatever kind of garbage eighteen-year old-boys dream between high school and college and he damn near ran across my legs. I think I may have yelped like a little girl. He was startled too and ran back to his den, spinning one-eighty now and again the way badgers do, torn between the urge to run from something big, or attack like the little prairie wolverine he was. He swam the ditch and dived into his den and then came out and looked at me. I left a dead gopher at the den mouth that day, starting a tradition. An apple for me. A gopher for Mister Badger. I have a total of about six people to talk to this whole summer—one of whom I'm pretty sure wants to kick the shit out of me—so I might as well make friends with a badger. I'm shooting the barrel out of Smith and Wesson .22 pistol that I bought new at old Meyer Hardware at the beginning of summer and killing gophers wholesale. I leave them where they fall, except for around lunchtime. Every day. I carry one by the tail and place it at the mouth of the den and go sit under the cottonwood. He almost always comes out.

This is what I do.

I shoot gophers, and water grass and alfalfa. This is about all I do. Except when evening comes, I walk down through the dust of the long road through the ranch to the river and I cast Daredevil spoons out into the Colorado. I like the red and white ones. Sometimes the black and white. But mostly red and white. Cast and reel. Cast and reel. I do not catch any fish, for the river is up and big and fat with brown silt. It has been this way the whole summer, from early June right through July. Only once in all of that casting do I have a strike, a rainbow trout that fights hard in strong current and spits the spoon right at the bank. I see a flash of red and green and it is over. But it is enough to keep me casting. It is always enough.

I read books too and the summer seems to go on forever. But mostly I drive along the Colorado River through the ranch where I am the only person irrigating hundreds of acres of grass. I drive and I shoot gophers. The ranch buys my shells. Or did until mid-summer when my shell bill at the little general store in Burns rang up to be about as much as they were paying me. Then they shut me down. I buy my own shells now. By the carton.

Three hundred dollars per month. Buy your own food. It's not

30

much of a salary, more like a bar tab. Somehow, I'm living on it. I eat a lot of apples and cheese and a lot of ten-for-a-dollar Ramen.

When I'm not driving the old pickup from one field to the next, I pull canvas check dams from one spot and place them in another. I walk through stands of young grass and alfalfa, a shovel in my right hand. My feet are hot and sweaty in hip boots rolled down and I clump through the grass and swing the shovel. There is a rhythm to my work, the swinging shovel slurping into wet soil, then clinking on dry clay. I bend to the field and dig a bit and water goes with gravity. The water muddy in the ditches and it bends around the steel of my shovel and washes against the mini-dams I create to quench the endless thirst of grass. The shovel is sharp and cuts sod cleanly and in the instant before the water comes, I see white roots and earthworms cleaved neatly, squirming. Then the water flows and all is brown and drinking. I find big dry spots out in the field and spend half a morning digging a little ditch to water five acres of grass that would die without the water. Die and become desert. All around the ranch are hills of clay and sage—desert. It is as if I am the last line of defense between the desert and Eden, between the ranch's winter hay, and sagebrush as tall as a man on horseback. Sagebrush and gophers.

They give me a house to live in, a white two bedroom under some cottonwoods. Mike lives there too and he smokes cigarettes late at night out on the concrete steps, listening to the hot breeze come through the cottonwoods. The cigarettes never go out. I'm not sure if I've ever seen him use a lighter or a match. He smokes down to a stub and lights one off the last one and keeps the fire burning.

Out there on the stoop, he smokes and he rubs the stump where his right hand used to be—a hand whose last act was fishing. Fishing cowboy style. In the first weeks, I did not ask about the hand that was not there and was so recently departed. But as time went on and as Mike decided the kid he was bunking with wasn't such a bad guy—and particularly as the beer started to flow—he told me. One night, drunk again, his words slurring like water over stone, he mumbled something about fuses and caps and shitty throws. These are technicalities that soar over the head of an eighteen-year-old boy with girls and trout on the brain. But I gather that the dynamite that he tossed blew up about a foot from the hand whose final move was throwing it—attempting to throw it—into a pond of big brown trout. Over the years, the pond had been slowly stocked, also cowboy style. Which meant when the river dropped in the autumn and the ditches fell, the trout that were trapped in shrinking pools—desperately darting from edge to edge in the main ditch—were caught a net-full at a time and carried in an old feed bucket to their new home in the pond. In the pond, though, the trout never lost their wild heart.

This was two months ago. Mike found the dynamite in the barn corner in a box thick with dust. The river was up and chocolate with spring and the catching not good at all. It was that slow time on a hay ranch when the water is not yet on and there is little to do but get ready for it. So the crew went fishing. Trouble was, the big browns in the little pond didn't get big by being dumb or easy to catch. Dynamite: the great equalizer. I have no doubt there was a little beer involved. I do not ask about the fish in the pond—whether the explosion that knocked Mike into handicapped parking for the rest of his life floated any big browns to the surface.

But I do wonder.

They drove Mike to the hospital in Glenwood. Drove like a bat out of hell, Mike propped up between Jim and Ken on the bench seat of the F-250. Mike held his shredded arm above his heart, a leather belt wrapped around the bloody remainder. His face bled and he could not hear anything. Could not hear the big V-8 growling under full throttle, could not hear the tires chirping and screaming around the canyon curves. Could not even hear when Jim and Ken yelled right in his face. His face was pocked with bleeding divots carved by bone chips—flying fragments of hand. There was no trace of that right hand.

Later that summer, the ranch manager asked Ken about a bill for seat covers. "Why you charging the ranch for seat covers for your truck?"

"Well Mike bled on them."

"No. We're not going to pay for that."

Ken shook his head. He's a big guy with a thick black beard and he works somewhere else on another of the ranches, probably the one up by Toponas, up on the mountain. I really don't pay much attention to what the others are doing. Except Mike and that's because Mike is right there. I don't know what he does except thoughtfully rub that stump at night under the dark cottonwoods. The night wind off the desert blowing through them, pushing the scent of sage and cigarette smoke into my open window. His hearing came back, but he mourns his hand. He comes back to the house late, driving his two-wheel-drive Ford into the yard in a cloud of dust. He's trying to learn how to shift and drive with a claw hand. They fitted him with it, a kind of hook apparatus that is supposed to open and close with the movement of his arm, but it is a clumsy thing and Mike—only a few months out from using the hand he was born with—hates it. It somehow makes me think of football shoulder pads with a claw attached on one end. He holds a red and white soft pack in that claw and fishes a fresh one out with his left, the dying butt in the corner of his mouth, squinting against the smoke in his eyes. He is a man in the middle of his life who without notice or practice must now learn how to use his other hand for the things that at one time had been automatic—signing a bill at the hardware store, lighting one cigarette before the last one burns out, brushing absently through thin hair, cleaning his glasses, casting a fishing lure. He is as clumsy as an infant at left-handed tasks.

One night, late, I am thrown out of bed, scared in the dark, by a crash against the screen door. I wait for a while and then hear snoring coming from the front yard, snoring and the occasional moan. When I peer out my bedroom window, I see Mike lying face up, his claw arm thrown to one side, sprawled in jeans and T-shirt, and hat lost on the grass. He had hit the screen door full force and now lay there, passed out. I rose and half carried him into his bed. He gets drunk with the ditch rider and his wife down the road. I have a very strong suspicion that he is taking the ditch rider's wife for a roll now and then. Late summer, the ditch rider, a small, friendly man, comes looking for Mike, who is somewhere else. When the ditch rider shows up, he is not friendly and he barks short questions and hardly waits for the answer before tearing off up the dirt road.

They call the one I'm scared of Oat. His name is Otis, but they call him Oat. This is how I see it spelled. Maybe he spells it Ot. He can spell it any way he wants to.

The first time I met Oat and his brother Jim and the whole family that lives in the other ranch house two miles up the road, they were all down fishing at the river. Drinking beer and fishing. I drove into the ranch and my new summer job as the sun was sagging west, miles of Colorado behind me. I stepped out into the smell of sagebrush and river mud. They were friendly, Jim and Myra and the kids. Jim offered me a beer. Oat glanced up at me from his fishing pole and waved his chin at me.

He's in his mid-twenties and I make him as puppy-kicking mean from the get-go. He doesn't say much, his countenance matching his black hair. He's wired tightly in frame and attitude, an average sized man, but strongly made, stretched tight like rawhide. I doubt that there is a sliver of fat on his whole body. Oat and his friendly brother are flatland eastern Colorado boys, now working on a high country ranch far away from any kind of supervision or management. The river ranch where I work is new to the company that owns it. Jim uses this freedom from bosses to work hard. Oat, I think, uses it to get meaner. Not that he needs any practice. I am learning a lesson I do not know yet, that some people get mad and bulletproof when drunk and others get happy and others weepy. The ranch is home to all of them. And the mean drunk wants to kick my ass.

I do not know why. Perhaps it is because I showed up on the ranch this summer without his approval. Perhaps it is because my job is a carefree one of driving dirt roads and watering grass and dreaming ridiculous teen dreams. Perhaps it is because I am going off to college in a few months and Oat never finished college and will be right here on the ranch—if he doesn't get fired—in a few months. More likely, he's bored and why not? We don't hit it off.

One day I am at the horse pasture a couple of miles upriver. It is a lovely place of green grass and cottonwoods where the Colorado comes out of a minor canyon and is met with a bank-to-bank tributary carrying snowmelt off Flattop. The trib runs full and brown all summer, for it had been a good snow year and the water lasts a long time. At the end of the summer, the little stream carries ash and charred needles from a large forest fire upstream, but the rest

34

of the season it is thick and silt-brown. The fire causes a momentary sensation at the ranch, a tinge of excitement during a long dull summer. For three weeks, we drive out into the desert, drop the F-250 into four-low and climb a steep hill where we can watch it. We drink beer and see the smoke and flames turn from gray to black when the fire takes aspen instead of pine. It slows then, but then flares up and the smoke grays and billows like a huge thunderhead born on the mountain.

The horse pasture is my favorite place, but there are no horses there. I make excuses to linger when I walk the little place. Its fields fall off sharply to the river and I wonder about the long-ago tough work of carving pastures and hay fields out of sagebrush-blanketed slopes. There are several old log buildings melting slowly into the clay and I wander through them and look for things like square nails, old bottles and rusted tin Log Cabin syrup cans shaped like little homes. I drive the old International pickup from the headgate, where I check for debris, to another ditch where I turn the water loose. When I turn the wheel, water shoots out of the main ditch like some kind of freed animal. It rolls and pushes debris. Free. I feel free up here on this two-hundred-acre patch of grass on the far side of the river.

So I stay, seemingly far away from Oat. I watch the sky and I walk the ditches and I turn water loose and I shoot picket-pins with my new pistol. The day gets away from me and it is late afternoon by the time I roll back down the gravel road. When I get close to the main house, I see the red Jeep pickup trailing a huge cloud of dust and coming my way. A muscled arm comes out the window. It is Oat and I slow to a stop and lean out the window.

"Where the fuck have you been?"

"Up at the horse pasture?"

"Been looking for you all morning."

"Why?"

"You don't need to know that. You just need to work."

"Okay, well, it was a mess up there."

"I don't give a shit. That lower field is flooding everywhere. Don't ever do this again."

It is a while before I catch myself dreaming at the horse pasture again. I bend to my work, stung. I throw myself at it and try to keep ahead of the endless thirst of grass. I even try to get the pasture across the river going, a pasture that Oat and Jim had abandoned for lack of time and help. I drive the old tractor over there, across the rickety wooden bridge, and I attempt to dig a long ditch from a fickle little stream out into the parched field. The clay here is cracked and reminds me of the way a thin bar of shop soap is lined with crevices of dirt from lathering many hands. In the end, this little project is too much, even for an earnest kid whose ears still burn from an Oat scolding. I leave the far bench to the desert because the main pasture is coming strong and needs water. It always needs water. I have work to do and I do not want to get my butt beat, so I put to it. Most days, I skip my dreamy lunches under the cottonwood and the badger skips a catered gopher meal.

Sometimes, I straighten from my shovel work and stretch my back and look up at Flattop and think about fishing and then I go back to it, walking the fields, swinging the shovel. Only occasionally leaning on it, just long enough to look at those cool blue pines up there. I still fish in the evenings, but it is usually too late to see a fly on the water, so I cast my Daredevils out into the growing darkness, into the thick strong current. Cast and reel. Cast and reel.

Jim breaks the monotony of it in late summer.

"Let's go camping. All of us. We'll take your truck."

The old International is the only pickup on the place that has a working four-wheel-drive. My friend Ken and his F-250 has been run off by the ranch manager. I do not know the details of his departure, only low overheard comments between Jim and Myra about Ken being told by the ranch manager to stay away from one of the women on the upper ranch and not heeding that order. So now, down here on the river ranch, my truck is the only truck that can get us to the mountain. It is a good old truck and if we really squeeze, we can fit four across and the kids in the back.

It is late afternoon the next day when I drive to the upper house, my bedroll thrown into the truck bed, rolling loose back there with a few canvas dams and spools of wire and my shovel. I put my fly rod back there too, cased in an aluminum tube. It is a beautiful thin thing, and although the case protects it, I worry about it back there with the shovel and gear. I haven't had much of a chance to use it this summer, but there are ponds up there on the mountain and brook trout in the stream. Mike told me about going up there last summer, back when he was a two-handed man, and catching a mess of fat, foot-long brook trout. Enough for a couple of fish dinners. Mike says he won't be going up there and I wonder if maybe it is because the mountain will make him remember a time when he was right-handed instead of a forced lefty. More likely, it is the prospect of having me out of the house and the ditch rider's wife just a few miles down the road.

Myra and Jim and the kids pour out of the house and bedrolls and a huge canvas tent and coolers and beer and bags of chips are all thrown in the back. There is a flurry of excitement and then Oat comes out of the small cabin where he lives, a duffle bag thrown over one shoulder, his hat pulled low over his eyes. He has a chew in and he spits and looks hard at me soundless and slings the faded green canvas duffle into the back in one fluid motion. There is an easy athleticism to him, the rawhide all working in perfect symmetry.

Oat drives. Myra and Jim pile into the front seat. Jim takes shotgun where he can open wire gates as we drive up the mountain and Myra spraddles gear levers and pulls tabs off beer cans for Oat and Jim and herself. Back in the back, propped up on sleeping bags and duffle bags, the kids—Mary and her little brother Pete—and I laugh and let the desert breeze rattle off of us. Pete wears thick glasses and his own straw hat and he holds it down on his head as we head off down the gravel and then grind slowly up the mountain road, switchbacking and laughing. It is good to be in the back with the kids and it reminds me of sitting at the kid table during Thanksgiving. It's a good place to be. Especially with Oat at the steering wheel.

It is dark by the time we turn off the main road onto a little jeep trail. The jeep road will take us up a long cramped canyon, climb the canyon's walls, and twist higher onto Flattop. Up there, up where it's cool and there are trout. We crawl slowly up the road, bouncing over rocks and splashing through little streams, old Blue the International growling in Granny. There is no breeze in the hair, but it is cool now and for the first time all summer, a long summer, I pull on a jacket against the mountain air. It smells of aspen and pine and willow and trout stream up here and Mary and Pete snuggle down into the softness of bedrolls and gear. Both edge up close to me now as we hunker behind the cab and bounce along.

It takes an hour or more to gyrate up the canyon. The road is narrow and rough and mostly one truck wide. There are no places to pull off for camping and so we climb. Higher and higher on the mountain until the sage gives way to lodgepole pine and we reach a high basin that widens before us. The canyon is peeled open into a hanging valley cleaved by the stream. But it is too black to see much except what is in the headlights of old Blue—they brighten and dim with the throttle.

After an hour of bumping and tossing about in the bed of the truck, it stops and the three adults lurch out of the truck. I peer up over the roof of the cab and into the black. In the thin light of the truck's headlights, I can see where the road goes into the stream—and lots of water. It is almost a pond and we all thumb flashlights out into it, looking for the far bank, sending beams of light into the thick water, trying to gauge its depth.

"I don't know, Oat."

Myra is the voice of reason, perhaps a bit less drunk than her husband and brother-in-law.

Jim grins. "Oat, we can do it, just get a run at it."

Oat nods. "Yep."

Myra looks at me, and then at the kids. Mary, Pete, hop down out of there. Oat is going to drive across.

Oat climbs in, grinds reverse and the truck growls backwards up the road and then revs and then there is a burst of energy and it leaps forward, Oat grabbing gears and Jim hooting loud and drunk. Blue launches out into the water while five of us stand and watch and a huge sheet of water splashes over us and the truck engine screams and then gurgles and dies. The water is nearly over the hood of the old four-wheel-drive and Oat grinds on the starter and somehow it coughs alive again and the exhaust pipe blubs into the water and Oat slams into reverse and Blue gamely lurches backward and gets almost out, but mud grabs and she starts to sink.

Oat desperately rocks forward, but the tires spin and the engine screams and then quits.

Stuck. Oat opens the door and water floods into the cab, a foot or more. He staggers through the water and sits on the bank, cussing and shaking his head. Myra hands him his beer.

"Better shut off the lights." Oat is looking at me.

I wade out into the thick dark water and it is up over my knees, reach into the open door, and shut off the lights.

More orders. "Grab that shovel and jack. Start digging."

We have a high-lift jack in the back, one of those jacks that creak dangerously upward, high enough to scare the hell out of you and tall enough so we can stack rocks under the truck's tires. Myra and the kids scramble off into the darkness with flashlights and come back dragging alder and aspen logs, some six-eight inches thick. Jim jacks and we cram logs and rocks and brush under all four tires. Oat smokes cigarettes on the bank and flips butts out into the dark water and pulls the tab on another beer and flips the tab out with the butts.

We work in dark water, wet and thrashing and though it is still summer, it is chilly enough. Beams from flashlights alternately held by Myra and the kids dance on our labor and our shadows undulate against the sides of the old truck. When we have done the last wheel, the driver's front, slopping around to the thighs in the water, Oat stands and flips another butt out into the water and hoists a can to his lips. Drains it and throws it into the bed of the truck.

"Let me try it."

Blue splutters, runs. Dies. Again. The truck roars and water and muck shoot out the tail pipe and Oat guns it and it screams unmercifully backward and the rear tires claw the sod on the far bank and then it sinks again. Again, Jim and I push slowly down on the jack handle, and again Myra and the kids wander off into the black and come back dragging gray logs and brush.

This time Blue lurches onto the bank, backward.

"I'll get a better run at it."

"No. No. Let's just camp here."

Myra backs her husband. "Yeah, Oat, the kids are tired."

They argue around it for a bit. Oat wants to try it, to get higher on the mountain. Finally, he gives.

We sleep that night in an old Army canvas tent, all of us. I sleep on a far wall, careful not to bump into the center pole that can bring the whole tent tumbling down. I walk carefully around Oat, even up here on the mountain. He stays up a long time by a campfire we build in the little meadow where we have stopped.

Morning reveals. The stream we thought we were crossing is actually an old beaver pond, its dam going back to the earth. On the far bank, the two-track road we were following is very dim and overgrown by young aspen and alder. This is the end of the road. In the night, we couldn't tell that. We eat breakfast and I uncase my fly rod.

The stream is small, so tiny that even Pete, with his short legs, can clear it. But it runs clean and deep in meadow soil, between clumps of red alder and willow. It smells of rich black mud and decaying aspen leaves and the sun comes up over the mountain and warms us. My jeans are still wet from last night's bath in the old pond and it feels good to warm in the sun and stand in the curling smoke of the campfire that Jim feeds to a roar.

There is a pre-fall feeling to the morning, cool, hinting of frost and of aspen leaves changing. Up here, up high, the grass has mostly turned yellow and it tans the hills, splashed in the slanting warm light of the coming sun.

The heat rises in the morning and the pond steams and I rig up my fly rod while Jim and Oat and the others grab poles and Cope tins full of earthworms. We scatter.

I walk for a while, alone, listening to the morning rising strong now, birds singing everywhere and over my shoulder, fading, the sound of the kids laughing with their mom. Morning's rising fast and the stream wakes, bugs rising from the water. Mayflies mostly, but the mosquitoes are up too and buzz around my ears and chew on my arms.

The stream in the little valley curves and slows in a series of old beaver ponds, gray stacked logs fronting on new meadows that once were deep water. The dams held spring silt back and slowly back-filled and sprouted grass. As I go up the stream, though, the meadows turn to shallow ponds, and then to deeper ponds and then I am at a new pond, deep. Its dam is made of new aspen, chewed sharp yellow by beaver teeth, the thin green edge of cambium showing against the yellow cut and white bark. The water squirts out in a thousand small water falls and from this little stream is a pond an acre in size or more.

Trout are hitting the surface of the pond now, taking little mayflies, and I pull out my small fly box from the button flap of my shirt and tie one on. A Royal Coachman and then I'm casting, letting the line sing out and into the water and it lands perfectly. There's a splash and I set the hook and a head-shaking fight, briefly and it's a brook trout ten inches long. I unpin the little trout, wiggling wet in my hand and I admire his spots of blue and red, his fins edged in white and I break his neck on an aspen log and thread a willow stick behind his gill plates and stand to cast again.

I cast like this, hardly moving, catching brookie after brookie. It is almost too easy and it pulls me in, deep. There is only the cast and the catch and the brief head-tossing fight, and the trout released or killed and strung for dinner on the willow stick with his dead companions.

I do not know how long I stand like this and cast and throw line and I do not know how long Oat sits there, behind me, watching. I am almost simultaneously aware of the scent of cigarette smoke on an upstream breeze, and the feel of eyes watching me. I jump and spin and he is sitting there, smoking, his fishing pole in one hand, a beer next to his outstretched legs propped up against a sagebrush.

"Hey Oat."

He doesn't say anything at first, and he stubs out his cigarette and squints at me. Then, "Been catching them haven't ya?"

"Yeah, I've got eight for dinner."

"Good."

It is almost a compliment. Almost.

"You want to get in here, I mean, I can move on up the stream. It's a good place."

"No. I'll watch you."

I go back to my casting, suddenly very conscious of getting it right, very aware when to strike. I catch a few more and Oat lights another cigarette. I don't want to turn around much, but his eyes on my back burn.

There are more fish, little ones. I let them go.

"I know where a big one is. He wasn't interested in worms."

I turn, surprised. "Really?"

"You want to try him?"

"Okay."

He rises and waves his head downstream. "C'mon."

I follow him back toward the truck and camp, perhaps a mile distant, and watch as the good beaver ponds, the good fishing holes, fade and are filled and become meadow again. These are all places I walked past as I came to better water, all places I did not fish.

Oat stops at the edge of an ancient beaver dam, and points below the old dam. The stream foams white over the edge of the old dam and into a big pool, perhaps a dozen feet in circumference. The pool is filled with old trees, for it was once a beaver pond as well, and when their roots were flooded, they died. They fell. Some stood.

"Right there, behind that root ball. There's a big one there. I saw him."

I crouch low and peer into the water where a spruce tree fell, leaving a deep hole at the end of a tangle of gray roots. The water bends around the roots, curving current and I see a flash of white down there deep. Look hard. The white becomes the edge of a fin and it is attached to a good trout. Another brook trout. A big brook trout. Huge. Maybe fourteen inches?

In the water, I can see the fish flash in the depth, taking some kind of bug in the deep water.

"See if you can catch him. I put a worm right on him. Not in the market."

"Okay."

In the old pond above, I can see thin trails in the mud where caddis have pulled themselves along, toting their tube-homes. There is a gold ribbed hare's ear stuck in my hat. I can remember my uncle tying it and sticking it up there. I've never used it. It is more like a prize than a trout fly. But it looks enough like those caddis in the mud and I twist it off the hat, the barb catching cloth and then coming free. My hands shake a little bit.

There is no room here among dead reaching tree branches, for much of a cast, so I just sling it, a pendulum of line and leader only as long as I can lift my arm and the little rod and drop it into the current. The fly catches water and pushes around the root wad and into the deep hole where I saw the white fin edge and there's a flash and a heaviness and I lift it into solidness and then liveliness. The trout surges, plows deep and I can feel his head shaking and I let him shake and don't give him any line and he tries to root-ball me and I keep him out of that mess somehow and he splashes hard on the surface, then shakes and dives again and then it is over and he is in my hand. Green and gasping and blue and yellow and red. Oat is there at my elbow, looking at the fish.

He thumbs back his hat and slaps me on the back.

It surprises me and his eyes bore into mine.

"Nice fish."

He smiles.

Meet Mister Brown

It is August, that thick season of harvest and summer fading in a series of hot days, a time of sunburn and sweat. Hay bales are bucked onto slow-moving pickup trucks grinding along in low range, and you think about going to the mountain to get away from the heat, or at least to cut a load of firewood. August means gather and get ready. Fall is coming and you find yourself squinting up at the mountain through the sweat and remembering places where you saw bull elk and buck mule deer last fall. Tall backcountry, away from roads and people and in wildlife heaven. Better shoot the aught-six a bit.

One summer afternoon, work slows when a lightning storm swells over the desert and big globs of water spatter across the bug-stained windshield of the old Ford. The storm drops enough water to wet the downed and unbaled hay and it stops work entirely. You grab a rod and head for the hills. There's a stream that comes down out of a limestone canyon, pooling and dropping, dancing between man-sized white boulders. Some of the holes are deep, so deep you can't see the bottom. Looking down into that indigo depth, something like fear edges into your heart. The stream is not large, but is depth is formidable. There could be anything down there.

You try lures at first, drifting spoons out into the pool, letting them drop down out of sight, a little silver glitter in a sea of deep, dark blue. Winking diamond-like, then star-like. Then out. When the line stops, you start to bring in the lure, and it rises from the depth, swings into the current, and comes on. You do this for a while, and you catch a few decent rainbows, enough to feed the hay crew a good supper. You kill them quickly and clean them in the cold water of the stream, pushing a thumb up the bloodline against the spine, thinking of fresh fish for dinner and of cold streams. You thread them through the gill plate onto a willow branch and place them in the cold water of a side channel. There's the smell of hay on your jeans and shirt, but your hands smell of fish. Not a bad thing.

Upstream a mile or two, there's a place where a huge pool is formed at the tail of a small waterfall perhaps three feet in height. During the spring, this place boils and rolls with big water and the waterfall is gone, but now, late in the year, it is there, lipping over the white limestone, dropping into the pool. This is the place where you lost a good Rapala last summer during the same kind of hay meadow respite. That darned lure had cost five dollars. It felt like a snag at first, but in the big clean pool, there couldn't be much to snag on. Then the line had started to move and your rod bent double and you cranked, hoping the eight-pound line would hold up, that something as stupid as a poorly tied knot wouldn't be the end of it. The fish had stayed deep and didn't seem to tire much. It swam and pulled, but didn't make any big runs. Instead it was more like an anvil swimming around down there out of sight and when you finally had enough, when your arms couldn't take it any more, you made one hard strong pull. It had been sufficient and the fish surfaced long enough to be seen and to see you. There was a tremendous splash, and then it was gone, and so was that five-dollar lure. Broken swivel. A two-cent part causes the lost of a five-dollar one. Kind of like ranching. You had seen enough though, a butter-yellow slab of a side, a hooked jaw, a mouth big enough to eat ducklings. Five pounds? Ten? No telling. Besides you aren't good at that anyway.

That kind of thing is hard to get out of a fella's brain, hard to erase. You have flashed to it all year long, memory and dream. Now it is another year, and you've got another five-dollar lure in the box you carry in your shirt pocket.

The hike up there is not long, but you step carefully. The canyon belongs to things that bite and sting—rattlers and poison ivy and stinging nettle. It's almost as if they are guarding the fortress of Mister Brown. You take all the right precautions and find yourself at the tail end of the deep pool where you rig up that new lure and weight it down and cast it out there into the black water where you can watch it sink for a long time until it winks out. Then you start a slow retrieve. Cast. Retrieve. Cast. Retrieve. Nothing.

Finally, you go to the backup, two thick night crawlers coiled in black soil in an old Skoal tin from your other shirt pocket. You thread the nightcrawlers onto a hook, feeling them squirm at its stab, and you tie the whole works down with a heavy weight and make a big cast into the deep pool. You watch the line as it feeds out, catches the current and starts to swing out. The line has all of your attention, and then it stops and you lift the rod into something solid and fearsomely heavy. It feels just like last summer felt. There's muscle memory there, the weight of the fish transferred through the rod to your forearms.

This time, you have learned from your mistake and you wait a long time as you reel and give line. No need to hurry it. The fish fights deep and fights slow and finally, you feel as if you are gaining ground. In the absolute clarity of the water, you can see him now, swimming deep, a long black form in the depth of it, and you pull hard on the rod, trusting the line and not using a two-cent swivel this time. The fish follows the pull of the line, and you have him close now, close enough to net him. You reach out with the net and start to slip his long head into it.

For a minute there, you make contact, your eyes and his. That cold eye. That is enough. One connection and he gives one last big shake of that hooked jaw and everything comes loose. You dive forward with the net, almost going into the drink, but it is too late. A head-shake, a flick of that big tail. He's gone. Back into the depths of the pool. Back into your dreams. Stored there until next year.

So long, big man.

Black River

Dad described it in detail. How his eyes changed. How it was quiet. How it felt lonely. He didn't say as much—that last part—but his words relayed it. The depth of it, the emptiness of sitting by a hospital bed as your father dies. Takes his last breath. It is cliché, the taking of the last breath, but this is what Dad described and this is the reason the room got quiet. His father took his last breath. Sometimes clichés are far more apt than a more creative attempt to capture the moment.

He is a calm, gentle, extraordinarily generous man, my father. An optometrist who grew up in small mountain town Colorado during the Great Depression. And he is describing his own father's death to his youngest son who is far off in college, miles away physically. Metaphorically.

He allowed himself a bit of silence then, over the phone. He usually holds himself tighter. But then he laughed at the imagined reaction of his own father, learning his wife is pregnant at the outset of the crash of the stock market. Forty years old and a baby coming and the economy in the tank. The farm out on the flatlands wasn't cutting it and when an opportunity came up a trade was made—a farm by Greeley for a summer cabin business in Estes Park at the edge of Rocky Mountain National Park. And so this is where Dad learned and lived and scrubbed cabin floors and cleaned up after rich tourists. The only tourists in the Depression were rich ones it seemed; those who had expendable cash were rare.

And now his own father, 90 years old, is gone.

A picture of my grandfather hangs in my dorm room. 1922. He's a young man and he is leaning on his bar next to his business partner. He owns the pool hall, the bar, the bowling alley in the back that you cannot see in the picture and he stands as if he does—arm stretched out over the cherry wood, hair slicked back. The silent authority of ownership in his shoulders. Greeley, Colorado, 1922. The Volstead Act is two years old, but liquor probably passes across that bar regardless. Behind him, fading into the background, are row upon row of pool tables. Men sit along the walls, balancing pool cues upright loose-handed. Some of the men's features are blurred in camera shutter time, bobbing, perhaps, to spit in brass cuspidors. Other men bend to the tables, aiming crook-armed, chalk-fingered. "If you can't pay, don't play" says a sign above my grandfather's head.

He was a logger, a farmer, a teamster, a sugar beet factory worker, a carpenter, a pool-hall-and-bowling-alley proprietor, and a summer cabin owner. Now he is gone.

I sit on the single bed in my dorm room, the cord from the phone slapping absently against my leg and I talk to Dad about things. Then we talk logistics and he tells me not to come home. "It won't matter anyway, you should stay in school."

We try like this for a while, brief, strange conversation that floats in the room, awkward. Stilted.

Grandpa. We were never close. He seemed to always be old. Old. Sometimes sick. But I wanted to know about his life, so I sat him at his kitchen table when I just barely into my teens and recorded his life on cassette tapes. It was not a school project. It was just curiosity. His was a life that started in 1890 and bent to hard work, a life that got through a time when there was nothing to do but get through. No time for frivolities. There are no fishing rods in his garage, no golf clubs in the trunk of his car. There is one shotgun, and it is spare and practical, a single shot 12 with a hammer trigger. He may have gone pheasant hunting down on the Greeley farm with it, but he doesn't talk of it. He does tell me of mowing hay with a two-handed scythe, swinging rhythmically, and flushing a nested hen pheasant. She launched, and he swung fatefully, accidentally, cutting her legs off and knocking her out of the air. He carefully gathered the eggs she had been sitting on and cupped them against his stomach in his work shirt. A farm hen hatched the pheasant chicks. Grandma and Grandpa ate that hen pheasant. Practicality. If mine is Generation Play, theirs—his—is Generation Hard Labor.

That picture though…there's something there that is confident and stoic. Rugged. Like his palindromic name. Otto. German. Strong.

"Okay," I finally say. "I'll stay down here."

My roommate offers clumsy condolences. He grew up in the desert city, a local Phoenix boy who knows little outside the palm and orange trees, the swimming pools. We are not close. George, the Ohio farm kid down the hall, is better at it: "Want to go fishing?"

It is prophetic, somehow, that the name is Black River. It matches. At the rim, we shoulder backpacks. Pines up here, but down below, agave taller than the flat one-story dorm building where I live in the desert. Agave and alligator juniper and a river flowing out of the taller mountains, a river that is warm enough to wade in tennis shoes.

We drop from the pines, sliding over loose rock and thin soil, past cactus that threatens punctures in unprotected legs. Down. The backpack is heavy. Camping gear. A stove. Fishing gear. A twelve pack. Each. We are in college, after all.

George did the research. The stream has smallmouth bass, fish that swam upriver from the lake far below the reservation, down in the low country. Now they live wild in the river. "I have never caught a smallmouth bass," I say to George. "You'll love bass," he says. "I've caught a lot of them at home."

So we drop, clouds of dust washing into our faces, loose rock tinkling with gravity and finally, the river. It is really a stream with a river name, perhaps twenty feet across at the widest and very shallow there.

It looks like any trout stream I've ever seen back home in the Rockies, like any place I've ever hooked a brown or a rainbow from cold, clear water. This is warmer, clear water and George and I stand at the river briefly, then find a place to drop our packs from our sweat-wet backs and dig out fly rods from aluminum tubes.

I piece mine together quickly, jointing yellow fiberglass to ferrule, and string up the fly line. "What do you use for smallmouths?"

"Streamers."

"Shoot, I don't think I have any. You?"

George has some big streamers in his fly box and he gives me one, a crazy combination of blue marabou and silver tinsel, a fly as large as a fish itself. It feels clumsy out there, waving around in the air. A few tips are offered, and I work upstream now, wading wet between long runs, past pools that shine clear in desert daylight. I cast and strip the big blue fly, and nail a foot-long smallmouth. It fights hard, making runs, dancing on the end of the line and I bring it in. We need fried fish to go with our beer, so I kill it quickly and move on.

The river takes me for a while, the newness of a fresh river, fish and land. I walk past strange, almost human-like tracks of coatimundi, past sharp swords of agave. Sand and stone. I catch a few more fish, clean them quickly, then sit for a while. My heart really isn't in it.

Some have closer connections. I think about this for a time, about a man who lived in a time different than mine, who never took the time to fish unless he needed the meat.

I sit there on the white-washed carcass of an Arizona sycamore and I think about a man I knew through my tape recorder, who stands in black and whiteness in his speakeasy small-town Colorado pool hall, a young man with dreams ahead of him, a family that hasn't been realized yet. A future ahead.

It occurs to me then, beside a Black River full of black bass, that my grandfather and I had more in common than I thought. He could have gone anywhere in the Great Depression. A big city, perhaps. Could have stood in the famous soup lines, or worked jobs in factories. Instead he chose the West, the high country, a small town. He scraped by where the mountains shone against the western horizon, where high snow dusted the peaks in early August, where streams of trout and parks of elk were never far away. He kept that connection to the land later on—a big garden in the backyard. When they packed up and left that house with the big garden for assisted living, he was gone in months.

And it is here that I realize we had the same thread in our lives— that of land and wild country and wild trout. He may never have carried a shotgun or a rifle or a fly rod just for the fun of it out into that land, but the land was there and that was enough. The common bond of Western towns, open country not far away, the land. That is the thread that runs through our shared blood like a thin tight fly line thrown out over the water into a river of wild fish.

Worm Dancing

Iola, Colorado. Don't look for this place on any modern highway map. You won't find it. It is dead and buried beneath one hundred feet of Blue Mesa Reservoir. But there once was an Iola.

It was the destination and June 12 was the date.

Any June 12, any year. June 12 meant the beginning of The Hatch. Not any hatch, but the Gunnison River willow fly hatch. The big one. Iola—never more than a few resort buildings and a post office—was ground zero of the hatch. Willow flies, also known as salmon flies and stone flies, are large, strange-looking bugs that spend most of their lives not as flies but as larvae beneath the surface of the water.

But on June 12, every June 12, the larvae got the urge. The same urge as bulls in September, bucks in October, boys at a Denver strip joint. Like some tiny, prehistoric creature, the bugs crawled out of the water onto a convenient rock, then slowly, surely, began to dry in the warm June sun. Soon, the material that was the skin became hard, fragile—a shell. The little bug inside the shell pushed against it, forming a crack. A little crack at first, too small to be seen, but the crack widened as the bug pushed. Finally, the crack was big enough to crawl through and an orange fly two and a half or three inches long crawled out, leaving the discarded shell behind.In the sun, the bug would dry its wings, fan them, pump fluids into them. As it dried, it took on color, a bright, hunter orange. Before long the black and orange flies swarmed out of the river, looking—like those bulls and bucks and boys—for mates. And the trout in the river below looked to eat.

And the fishermen who came to Iola from Denver and Chicago and San Francisco caught. Rainbows mostly, but some king-hell browns drew the fishermen to the Gunnison River in the first half of the 20th century. It was a river like few others in the West for several reasons. First, a railroad paralleled its banks. Second, the Gunnison was a unique combination of high country stream in fertile ranchland. The waters were very cold, perfect for trout, but the air above was warm and ideal for growing such trout food as willow flies. Third, the railroad and the trout gave rise to resorts. Resorts galore. And with the bustling, growing city of Denver only a few hours away, the resorts and the tourist business hatched. No other river in Colorado compared. The resorts became famous: Black Canyon Resort, The Rainbow Hotel, The Sportsmen's Hotel, Rippling River, Jointed Rod, Coopers, Neversink....They all sank in the 1960s.

That Gunnison is gone. I will never fish its waters or see what it looked like. Instead, we have the Lower Gunnison. It is my Iola. One hell of a river it is. Water. Water is the West's oil. The 1960s were the era of the big dams and the dams that claimed the Gunnison—collectively called the Curecanti Project—created a river fishery where none had been. Before Curecanti, the lower canyon, commonly known as the Gunnison Gorge, was not a trout fishery. It was a warm, slow, sucker-filled river rolling westward for the desert.

Then along came the dams. First Blue Mesa, then Morrow Point, then Crystal. The water that comes out of the last dam is as pure and cold and rapid as a high country river, but it is in the desert. For miles, it flows past ponderosa pine and juniper and piñon, bending around steep canyon walls, carving into granite and sandstone, shoving huge piles of sand onto the banks. In the riffles are the rainbows, but in the deep pools above and below are browns. Rainbows, though, rule the river and it is for these green and red and black beauties that most fishermen come. The Gunnison Gorge is a rainbow river. Several trails lead down off the canyon lip to the river. Duncan, Chukar, Ute, a handful more. Some people opt to scramble down off the canyon lip at odd points, but this is a dangerous proposition that promises to rip a hole in your waders at the very least. Farther up the canyon is a place where a friend's friend fell several hundred feet to his death while he was coming up the canyon after a day's fishing. I stick to the trails. It would be easy to say that a trout river in the desert is incongruous, but that's simply not true anymore. In today's West, desert trout rivers are the norm. The San Juan below Navajo. The Green below Flaming Gorge. The Colorado below Glen Canyon. The Big Horn below Big Horn. And the Gunnison below the Curecanti system. This is the legacy that has been left to us who fish for trout by those hungry for hydropower and irrigation water. It is not a cruel inheritance. In fact, fishing those desert rivers can be a beautiful experience. It is modern fishing and probably the future of fishing.

As much as I may miss those rivers that I never knew, I'll be the first to admit that I benefit from the rivers that were born as the result of those canyon corks. I know the new rivers. The first time I saw the Gunnison Gorge was a warm late October day. We were up and gone before the sun was even thinking about getting up. There were four of us, men whom I'd never fished with, but fishing, unlike hunting, is something of a social sport. I'll fish with anyone, but I'm picky about my hunting partners. So the four of us headed west before light. Hours later, the canyon rim. The trail dropped steeply into the mouth, down past junipers and piñons, around clumps of sage. A horny toad, perhaps catching the last flies of summer, shuffled slowly across the path and the rising sun warmed my face and chest and got the sweat rolling. We scrambled over a small cliff where the trail became a route, easing our way down off the rim, careful not to knock rocks down on the man below. The route became a path and we kept going down.

Then the river. It ran clear and blue and cold before our eyes. The sun had not touched its waters yet and it rushed by in the darkness of the shadows, bound for its junction with the Colorado at Grand Junction. We stepped out of the sun into the shadow and made our way to the river, digging into day packs for waders and vests and fly reels. For a moment, I was embarrassed with my simple fly rod and cheap reel. The others were better armed. They had it all, from the brand-name rods worth more than my fishing car, to the beautifully crafted fly reels, to the boxes of compartmentalized flies. I pulled on my heavy rubber waders and dug a fly out of the film canister that I used for my flies while the three discussed water clarity and temperature and a probable pattern. The river beckoned and I waded into its cold waters, still marveling at the fact that I was in a desert, in late fall, fly fishing. I made a careful, cautious cast out into a riffle and immediately hooked a small rainbow. Another cast and another fish. I forgot all about my companions, shouted something about seeing them later and moved off down the river. I did not make it far. The first significant riffle I came to, I stayed in much of that morning. The water made a distinctive line as the faster part of the river met slower waters of the back eddy I was standing in. From eye level, the fast water was higher than the slow water. So I stood there, water curling around my rubber waders, and I cast into the same spot many times. I caught rainbows, each about the same size, color and vigor. It was one of those seamless and uncanny times when it seemed as if everything I did was right. And I never changed flies.

Prior to the trip, a friend had advised using a particular fly with a name that sounded like bait: the San Juan worm. I had never heard of such an animal, but I figured if it carried the name of the river and that river was a desert river born from a dam and the Gunnison was a desert river born from a dam....He showed me the fly before the trip and I laughed in his face. A hook with a piece of chenille. The world's easiest fly to tie. Mostly, it is tied in red or orange. A few patterns are chartreuse. So I stood in that spot with my San Juan worm—tied just the night before—casting from nine o'clock and drifting to three o'clock and doing it all over again. I probably made one hundred casts while standing in roughly the same area, but I wasn't doing it because I was lazy and didn't want to move down the river. I was catching fish. I'd cast, drift about a foot, then set the hook when my line stopped momentarily. A rainbow would be on, fighting the heavy current, fighting me, line zinging off my reel as it ran downstream. It was a rare experience. I lost count at twenty and gave up on the spot after the action slowed to one fish per half dozen casts. Other parts of the river were less productive, but I didn't care. By noon, I was well down the river, far out of sight of my friends. Once, a small raft stuffed with fishermen and a guide floated by, but that was all I saw of others. I found a huge old pine log high on the banks of the river and sat there to eat my lunch. It was warm in the desert and there was a light mayfly hatch on. The rest of the day, I worked back up the river, eventually finding my partners. One of them had snapped his rod on what he thought was one heck of a rainbow at the time. He hand-over-handed the line in to net the fish. It turned out to be a world record sucker. He was pissed that his expensive rod had given in for such a fish and he just glared at me when I offered him the use of my $50 hardware store model.

By mid-afternoon, I tired of catching fish and I lay on my back in the sand of the river, staring straight up into the sky. Clouds drifted by and I watch a raptor spin lazy circles. I napped.

Desert rivers, for all their charms—rattlesnakes, cactus, oppressive heat, flash floods—harbor something special: spring fishing. In the Rockies, spring fishing isn't much. There really is no springtime in the Rockies. It snows in June. Sometimes July. Gunnison, Colorado, one of the coldest spots in the country, has something like forty five frost-free days. It's not tomato country. But drive west and you discover springtime. On desert rivers. On a spring day in the Gorge, one is likely to see cactus blooming, feel the caressing warmth of the desert sun, hear canyon wrens stake out their territories, and catch fish. Not just any fish, but spawning rainbow trout. Fish so full of life and the season that males squirt milt all over you when you bring them to hand. On a Friday in May, I skip out of work, claiming the need for field time. My friend Jim meets me at the house with his truck, mumbling something about not being able to leave his dogs behind after looking into their hopeful eyes. In the camper shell, Ned and Jed grin, tails thumping wild against the pickup bed.

In the darkness, we pass dozens of deer browsing on the side of the highway. We drink coffee from a steel thermos and tell stories of other trips and other experiences. One of the reasons I like going anywhere with Jim, a retired game warden, are his stories, tales of investigative work. I don't hear the same one often and when I do, it is a good story to hear again. Those are the best kind.

The trip includes a ritual stop at a café, loading up on cholesterol. It is planting season and the café is packed with farmers. We slurp down more coffee, pay the detached waitress, and climb back into the cab. We wind through fields of recently planted crops, onto a back road to the desert. An orange and white tom cat leaps from a ditch and Jim brakes to miss him. Should have taken out that old pheasant killer, he grumbles. The road bends at a crop, crosses an irrigation ditch running full with the Gunnison, and bends again. Just as quickly, we are in the desert and the fields are behind us. The soil here is gray-blue, some of it completely barren, but most covered with sagebrush and rabbitbrush and greasewood. During a dry stretch, the soil is easy travel, but mix in a little water and you have a world class quagmire that will suck down even the best four by four. It is dry, though, and we push on. There are tiny, almost unreadable signs at the tracks that lead to the trails into the canyon and we turn on the first one, trying a new part of the canyon. At the trailhead, we unload among the junipers. Two other vehicles wait here and our hearts sink a bit, then rebound. It is a big river. We shoulder our packs—containing lunch, waders, vests—and traipse down the broad, well-maintained trail. Jed and Ned gallop out into it. At the river, we debate about which way to turn, then decide on upstream. The canyon is narrower here than downstream, darker, more forbidding. Upstream is the darkness of the Black Canyon of the Gunnison, a nearly-inaccessible maw in the desert, but we won't be going that far. I get a strike on the first cast, dead-drifting the intrepid San Juan down an eddy. I lift the rod, miss the fish, cast again. Jim works across the river, Jed bounding happily through the shallows, then swimming strongly for the far bank. Ned, the old timer, struggles against Jim, who grabs his collar and helps him along, holding his snout above the rushing spring-cold waters of the Gunnison. It is cold. The sun is still far behind the lip of the canyon. Even by mid-morning, it has not touched us. The bottom of the canyon only sees perhaps about two or three hours of sunlight this time of year. Jim and I chat as we swap turns casting into the current, going through the fly box. I switch from the worm to a woolly bugger, and then to a gaudy, unlikely creation called the girdle bug and back to the worm and then to a golden stone and back to the worm. Nothing. It is no big thing though, the fishlessness of it all. I am here for more than that. True, the fishing draws, gives an excuse to come out on a day in early May, but it is more. I'm not working. That's part of it. But so is the scent of the desert on the water, and my friend laughing at the day and his dogs. When Jim is up, both dogs stand attentively on the riverbank, staring into the waters of the river as if pointing out trout. Ned, especially, looks as intently at the waters as he does at a sage hen he has pinned down on the October sagebrush sea. Jim has no luck either.

After a time, we sit on a big, black rock polished by high water from years past. The rock is smooth and slick and the dogs scrabble to get a toehold on the glass surface, finally making it. Overhead, bandtail pigeons play in the current and we look hopefully for a peregrine falcon. They live in the Gorge, swooping like fighter jets among the cliffs, snatching pigeons, but we don't see them. Instead, we watch the pigeons drift in the air and admire otter tracks just below the rock. They lead into the water. River otters were decimated in the late 1800s by trapping and water diversion and habitat loss, but the state swapped other wildlife species with Oregon and now the otters once again swim in the Gunnison and several other Colorado rivers. The sun finally hits us and we warm quickly on our black rock, eating our sandwiches and petting the dogs. I tell Jim I was a little doubtful when he brought the dogs this morning, for I have known so-called fishing dogs who ruined a good fishing trip. But these will do. It is good to have them here, panting happily on sun-warmed black rock. We move on, cross the river again when we are cut off by a deep pool and a fearsome, soaring cliff. On the other side of the river, a vague path leads several hundred feet up above the canyon, bypassing a major cliff. We struggle up the trail in our waders. Jim keeps a sharp eye on his dogs. It is a long drop to the river. Then the trail sags to the river and he breathes less tightly and we come to the water again and cast. With the same luck. None. Not even a bump, and I begin to get discouraged. I am confident in the worm, but that confidence doesn't feel good on the dwindle-down. With fly fishing, a confidence pattern is one you hate to see fail. You have bragged on the pattern, told friends tales of the fish it has taken and is yet to take. But when it fails, it is like a champion boxer who goes to the mat under the gloves of a young punk. It is embarrassing, especially if your money was on the champ. We get serious about the fishing, splitting up, working the deeper pools, the shallow riffles, the pocket water behind the boulders. Nothing. Not even the tiniest of takes. I work upstream, around a bend. The canyon river calls and each bend is new, a page turned. I'm caught up in the fishing, but not so much that I can't take in the beauty of the place. At one major pool, dark, deep and probably full of fish, I cast and cast and cast again, working hard at the task. Finally, in frustration, I watch a water ouzel who has a nest of sticks and mud plastered into a crevice in the cliff face above the water. The water dipper skims low across the water, twittering wildly, hitting the water now and then and disappearing. He bobs and ducks and swims in the roughest places. Ouzels can dance out of crashing, crushing waterfalls, scrambling on the bottom of the river, digging at pebbles, catching caddis larvae.

For a long time, I stand in the slow current at the tail of the pool, just watching the ouzel, my fly line limp in the water beside me, some of it wrapped around my legs by the river. Gradually, I break out of my ouzel trance and work back downstream to Jim. I left my watch at home, but I can tell that the sun is leaving. Its warmth abandoned my shoulders hours ago. I move down the river, still casting hopefully, now just using the worm, as if the San Juan will come to the rescue. We leave the river, huffing up the steep trail to the truck. Up top, canyon rimmed, a group of river rats unload a big raft, exchange handshakes with their shuttle driver, and wave goodbye, moving off down the trail we just climbed, jostling the raft between them. Fishless on the Gunnison. I never thought I'd see it happen. But it had to eventually. Even the best rivers disappoint. The fishing. Not the river.

This time, it is another friend, one who is my age. He asks me about the day before. We didn't catch anything, but it was a good day, I tell him We are in my old Ford, humming steadily westward at an easy 55. I don't push the truck much faster, because of the rattles that forebode a falling apart. In the warmth of the cab, Mark pours cups of coffee and I tell him about the bandtail floats and the peregrine hope and the otter tracks and ouzel dips. I talk little of the lack of fish. We make the traditional stop at the café, more carbs. Even after back-to-back days of such food, there is no concern. The river and the hike will burn it off. Now it seems as if we are regulars there and our waitress, the same one who served us so stoically the day before pours coffee while asking about the fishing. She doesn't stick around for the answer. The river. We crest the hill, then work down to the rim of the canyon and over into its maw, anticipation quickening our steps. We scramble down rock fields, hop across a tiny spring rivulet, wind through juniper and sage and yucca and round a bend to see the river there. We've both seen it before, but we must stop. To keep walking and not pay attention to the river would be an insult to the coming day. So we pause and then push on faster. There is a run of water on the Gunnison that is like no other stretch of water on the river. It is probably thirty yards in length and I don't know how deep. During low water—which can be almost any time of the year—the entire volume of the river, which is kept at a minimum flow of three hundred cubic feet per second, pours through the run like water shooting down a garden hose. The rafters can't fish the run very well because it's a fast one. They have time for two casts and that's all. But wading, you can work the water the way it should be. Although it is a long way from the end of the trail, Mark and I head there ritualistically. If there are more people on the river, we park ourselves on the run. If not, we might hike beyond to other good runs or riffles or backwater eddies, saving the best for later in the day. More often, however, we'll work the run and then move downstream.

This time, we settle in at the run, me at the head, Mark at the tail. He casts, I cast. We're worm fishing, San Juan again. Mark hooks up almost immediately, battling a nice rainbow. I hook up, whooping, rod held high, reeling a fish to hand. We each admire our fish, then release them back to the current, casting again. In all, we work the fast riffle for more than an hour, casting, drifting, watching, setting the hook on fish and rocks. The action slows a bit, the fish made wise by our offerings or made numb from the sting of the hook. We mutually decide to move downstream where there is another good riffle, a place where the river bends as it hits harder, darker, older rock than the sandstone up the middle canyon. The darker rock looks the same to my amateur eye as the black rock of the Black Canyon upstream. At the rock, the river bends slightly west, creating a good pool. It's a fishy pool, full of trout.

Out of the corner of my eye, I see something slide off the bank and into the water and my brain fails to register what it is. Until, that is, I see three large rainbow leap completely, oddly, out of the water, a clean four feet into the air, an action that is as panicky as it is odd. An otter. Had to be an otter.

The pool proves barren of fish, or at least the trout are in no mood for eating when something else is in the mood for eating trout. I move on downstream, Mark above, working a likely-looking current edge. My friend is a master fly fisherman, although he doesn't make much noise about it. He casts with a grace that most never develop. We catch and release a few more trout, spawners. The males drip white streams of milt on our waders as we pull them from the water. The females, fat with eggs, are cradled gently in the water and released as gently. Go on, little mother, give us more fish.

Late in the day, the sun high over the desert, we sit on a streamside boulder and pry our lunches out of our vests. Mine is a soggy peanut butter and jelly sandwich lump. For a long time, we sit on the rock and soak up the sun and listen to the river. Then we move.

The rainbows are on their beds, slowly finning out a place to lay their eggs. Suckers, huge ugly bastards, are on the gravel bars too, perhaps gorging themselves on trout eggs. Mark and I take turns on the rainbows, sight casting above spawning fish and then working the San Juan worm down past them. Sometimes, we see a flash of a yawning white mouth and set the hook before the strike indicator can even move. Sometimes, we land fish, other times, we just watch. Catching fish off beds can be as destructive as the suckers, so we don't work too hard at it. Those fish that we do catch are released without ever coming out of the water. We watch several dart back to their home territory, their momentary adventure forgotten.

The day before ended with the empty wash of futility. This one ends because the fishing is too easy. We laugh for a time about the two days, and we look to the canyon rim. It is a long climb out.

Cochetopa

It's a lonely country, big, open, lost. Pines edge the huge mountain park and the La Garitas rise to the south, another of several twisted and tossed ranges that make up what most people call Colorado's San Juan. High country. Ten thousand feet above sea level. Mountains rising four thousand feet higher, cupping the high wide park.

Not many people go here. It is generally hard to get into. From the San Luis Valley side, getting to Cochetopa requires a trip over the Continental Divide, then back over the divide on a criss-cross hatchwork of washboarded dirt roads. Even from the Gunnison side, the park is isolated, a clean one hundred miles from the nearest stoplight in town.

It is worth the trip. There are elk in Cochetopa, a few decent trout streams, a fine buck mule deer or two and there's even moose. They were transported in by wildlife officials, but not the first one. That first moose was a young wandering bull, several hundred miles south of where he should have been up on the Wyoming border. A decade later and more moose came down, involuntarily loaded into horse trailers and driven southward.

There are antelope, too, in a high park spread out wide. Prairie goats at 10,000 feet. Perhaps they are drawn here. I am drawn here. More than 100 years ago, another young man was drawn to the park.

His name, if names mean anything at this elevation in a remote mountain park, was Jack Smith. Perhaps to prove that maybe names don't mean anything, he also had an alias: Jacob Sattler. No on knows why.

In 1881, Jack made his way into the mountains between the towns Saguache and Gunnison. They were wilder mountains then, on the edge of Ute territory, close to a mining district, bristling with trouble. Jack was part of a detachment of the Infantry Company G, U.S. Army. A soldier. He had been all of his life, serving in the Mexican War in the late '40s, then coming West.

But something that year set him off. He may have gotten lost as a newspaper speculated. He may have had enough of fighting. Or he may have decided that Cochetopa was a pretty good place to die. But something stopped him, made him put the muzzle of his Army-issue .45-70 to his head and send a huge chunk of lead through his brain.

The *Saguache Chronicle* wrote: "The said Jurors upon their oaths do say that the deceased came to his death by shooting himself. We farther [sic] find that the deceased was a soldier belonging to the Infantry, belonging to the company 'G'...

"There was nothing found near the body with the exception of the belt above referred to and an army musket and knife in a leather sheath. From information received from the acting Coroner it appears that the soldier had been out hunting and getting lost and probably nearly dead with thirst—there is no water in the vicinity of the place where the remains were found—had determined to shoot himself as the best way out of his misery."

Apparently when the Army found his body, they transported it down valley where a creek ran, as if the sound of water could quench that thirst in the afterlife.

One hundred seven years later, Jack turned up again. In the summer of 1988, a couple of fishermen were plying the waters of Saguache Creek in the Cochetopa when they found part of Jack sticking out of a bank that had been washed away in the spring floods. There he was, leg bones sticking out in the hot mountain sun. The fishermen called the authorities. The authorities, noticing that this particular body was not from 1988, or even from that century, called in other authorities and the mystery of Jack started to unravel.

On the skeleton, archaeologists found brass buttons, a spent .45-70 cartridge—perhaps even from the very same that did Jack in—the remains of a leather boot, the remnants of what was possibly his ammo pouch and eight square-headed casket nails. There was also a headstone with the barely readable letters: "Jack Sm" and part of an old pine casket.

They put Jack in a new box, hauled him to a good location with a great view of the soaring La Garitas, and reburied him with full honors courtesy of the Gunnison American Legion. Jack was back in the ground, hopefully for good.

Outdoorsmen have a funny way of stumbling onto stuff in the backcountry. Fishermen found Jack, but it was hunters who found another skeleton late in 1988 in Cochetopa. Again, no one knew the name of the man, but this corpse was a whole lot fresher. Like a couple-months-dead fresher. So the hunters, their quarry forgotten, scurried into town and reported it to the local authorities.

The man, it turned out, was dying. Near his remains, they found a tattered sleeping bag, a few cans of label-less food, a makeshift shelter made of plastic. And a colostomy bag. Like Jack Smith, the man had left something behind that would withstand the elements. Plastic. The bag said all it needed to say: cancer.

It was pretty clear what had happened. The man had come to the country to die. Drawn to it, perhaps from a childhood memory or a fishing trip as a teen. Or just perhaps because it was one of the few truly blank spaces left on the map of Colorado.

It has a pull, this place. A wide expanse of country, mountains everywhere, ponderosa pines and aspens and spruce and clear water running. There is a stream in Cochetopa, a stream that I can hop across in a running leap. The kind of crick that I would call a one-hopper. At my back rises a hunk of undramatic mountain known as Cochetopa Dome, while off in the distance ahead is Sawtooth Mountain, a soaring hulk, a fragment of mountain spit off the Continental Divide into the Cochetopa Plain. The fishing is excellent because it is catch and release only, flies or lures.

The soul of the fisherman is filled with special places like Cochetopa. Rivulets to streams, streams to rivers, time rolls on. But the heart of the angler remembers. It remembers places where sunlight slants to laughing water, it remembers perfect fish and precise casts and it remembers place. Years slip over life's smooth stone, and still the soul does not forget. It forms its own DVD in high resolution and everything is ready to play back—the laughter, the scent, the way a stream talks, the waft of sage on a mountain current. It's even there in your arm, muscle memory of a special fly rod and the weight of the line singing in thin air. Decades have passed and I am well north and have not returned and perhaps never will, but Cochetopa lives. It is no coincidence, I think, that to the ear the word nearly sounds like Utopia. Sometimes, when winter presses in, or when I wake in the middle of the night, I visit.

I am there again, young and full of myself, the cocksure editor of the town's only newspaper. One afternoon in a time that seems like just yesterday, I was determined to cast off memories of the office, to cast to browns and rainbows. But beckoned not by water, but place, and plane. That plane that is fly-fishing in wild, lonely lost country, a zone of complete absorption of consciousness into the "now."

And here it is: Streamside now and deer tracks dimple the mud, tracks leading out of the water and into the meadow. I slap impatiently at a mosquito whining in my ear, and cast gently, placing the fly down at the head of the pool where the fast current meets the deep hole and forms a visible boundary.

The fly bobs on the current and floats past my feet. I cast again and again, liking the feel of the sailing line, the power and control of the nine-foot graphite rod.

The water is slightly off from a recent rain in the high country and the fishing is slow. To the west, lightning flashes, severing the sky and touching down on the south edge of Sawtooth. Minutes later, I hear the rumble, like the sound of a dozen jets streaking to a faraway war.

I can smell the rain in the air and see it pelting the mountain to the west. But I fish anyway.

Daylight fades, greeted slowly by dusk at the door. There is still time to fish, to cast in the wind and place my fly where I can. The wind comes now, bringing the storm on its back. Lightning flashes in the west again and thunder follows, more quickly this time.

Several more casts and I give up on the pool and move through the deep grass and willows to the next bend in the creek. The water twists and turns through the meadow, meandering here and there, indecisive as to the best course.

I strip line, false casting, letting the lure of elk hair and feather dry in the rain-swollen wind. I set the fly down at the head of another pool, but less gently this time, slapping the water clumsily. The fly bobs and drifts, and begins to pick up speed, dragged by the fly line in faster current.

Disgusted at myself and the wind, I pluck the fly off the water and cast again, only to curse again. The wind up and strong now, gusts of it battering me face-on, taking the fly line wherever it pleases, the three-weight weak against the storm's muscle.

The fly has somehow grabbed a finger of the willow several feet behind. I work it loose and turn it over in my fingers, looking for a bent hook, a dulled point, or an unraveling of thread.

No harm done and I am happy with my work, work at winter's fly vise next to the woodstove while the wind and snow whistled outside. A fly tied with the hair of a cow elk that I shot the season before. Now, even though it is early August, I can feel the change coming once again, a change that always comes, no matter how hard I wish it wouldn't. In the next few weeks, I will ignore nature's changes and fish as much and as hard as I can, for this was the time of year that I dreamed of during the cold winter evenings, and even before then, when I bent to the warmth of the elk and admired her hide and thought that it was perfect for light caddis, size 16.

And now, Cochetopa. I move up to another pocket, a slick run of water between the wrinkled sheets of the shallows. This time the cast is perfect, leader streaming out beautifully and fly lighting softly on the surface. And this time, my cast is rewarded. There is a swirl of yellow, a sharp tug and a brief, but tough fight.

I kneel, admiring the brilliantly-colored brown, its red and black sprinkled sides and its power. I cradle the fish in my office hands, holding it back in the current. Its gills work, breathing life and with a flick of its tail, it is gone, back into the dark home beneath the undercut bank.

Overhead, a nighthawk cries its welcome to the dusk, zooming down through unseen insects. The bird, too, can probably feel the coming of fall.

The rain finally comes, not in a torrent, but giving the skin of the meadow a sponge bath, a gentle caressing. The smell of it—sage and pine and mud and fresh-cut hay on rain-wind.

Suddenly, the water at my feet turns a crimson-pink and I look up to see a brilliant fire of sunset on the shoulder of Sawtooth. The sky is deep pink, merging to violet. Tawny hills below, the day's final welcome to the entering evening.

The gentle rain, too, is splashed in crimson, fire raining down from the sky.

It begins to rain a little harder.

I reckon we all have our Cochetopa. I have several. They are born of meltwater and high snow fading. They etch our landscapes and seep through granite and limestone, laugh down canyons of lodgepole pine and alpine fir, wind and meander through sedge meadow and aspen grove, then drop to sage flats that in late summer swell with the chatter of grasshoppers. Mine are blue lines—thin as the cut of a razor, little more volume than a few fire hoses. It seems sacrilege to describe their waters in cubic feet per second, for these are birth waters where our trout are as pure as the snowmelt itself. In the highest holds of the Cochetopa are Rio Grande cutthroat on the east side of the Divide, Colorado Rivers on the west. Pure and native and as wild as they were when Jack Smith crested a sagebrush bench with his .45-70 slung over one shoulder. As those streams follow gravity, brook trout, then browns and rainbows. All wild—or perhaps if one is technical—feral. But all eager to rise.

These blue lines of cold water are all Cochetopa and their memory relief. I think that perhaps when we need to, we fishermen will conjure these places and the people. We will recollect places that sing, will rewind that song and play it again. And smile with the memory. Even if we never return, we can go back.

The Canyon

To me, it has been and probably always will be simply, The Canyon. Not just any canyon, but my canyon, for my footprints are often the only ones that etch its bottom and sides on any given month of any summer.

Getting to the rim is really no big deal—a highway, a dirt road, a rough four-wheel track. But once on the rim, it's easy to see why no one ventures into The Canyon. Harder, probably, to understand why I do.

There is no trail off the rim. There is a route, a dim track sprinkled with moose turds and grouse tracks, leading down, down, down.

Gravity pulls at you, slamming your toes against your boots, torquing your knee ligaments like some crazed rubber band in a child's toy. Some of the time you spend on your butt, sliding in the rubble of crushed rock. Other times, you chimney carefully down between boulders as big as mobile homes, knowing that a slip, a twist, will snap those rubber band ligaments and leave you in a hell of a spot.

It's a long way down before you hear what you came for: the river. Or, more correctly, what swims in the river.

Mountaineers have their mountains. Canyoneers have canyons. Some penetrate the canyons with rope and rappel gear. I go there with fly rod and reel and I let myself fall under the spell of vertical fishing.

At the base of The Canyon is one of the prettiest trout streams in the Rockies. The stream, usually shallow enough for hip boots or wet-wading, bounces this way and that in the bottom of The Canyon. The rocks squeeze the river unmercifully, but once in a while, they relent, letting the river breath out into a deep pool of crystal water. You can see the fish swimming there, finning, porpoising to take some kind of invisible insect. So you thread your line hurriedly, twisting on a reasonable facsimile of the bugs in The Canyon. And you cast.

The casts call for finesse and grace, two factors that sometimes leave you bumbling and stumbling and cursing. The trees and boulders hang out at odd angles, ready to grab your backcasts. But once in a while, you land a perfect one and a trout rises hungrily. You set the hook and fight a wild rainbow to your hand. You cast again, and it's a brown this time.

Once, I sat at the tail of the pool, not moving, letting the water spin-cycle around my legs. From that spot, I caught and released five fish in a row. Each cast brought a strike and each trout I brought to hand and released. A brown, a rainbow, a skinny brookie, then another rainbow and another. Each as wild and as hard fighting as the one before.

Another summer at the end of the same pool, I found the weathered, bleached remnants of a seven-point elk antler. It rested on a sandbar, covered in lichen, forgotten, going back into the earth that birthed it.

There are other animals in The Canyon too. I've seen their tracks, their sign. Late one afternoon, side-hilling above the river, I backtracked over my own path taken early in the morning. In the fine dust where I could read my tracks, I saw others stamped on top of them—a signature saying "This is my canyon." I studied them for a long time before I realized what they were, rounded, padded. My heart pounded in my ears with the discovery. The mountain lion followed me up The Canyon, probably watching as I cast and caught fish, then peeled off when my scent came wafting downstream. I slept a little uneasily that night, my sleeping bag jammed against a boulder on a reasonably level spot.

Possibly because no one goes there or perhaps because sunlight hits the bottom of The Canyon only for a few hours each day, the trout rise easily to what I offer. I've never failed in The Canyon. I've emptied whole fly boxes, looking for patterns that have never caught fish, just to say I've caught something on that fly. Even a huge salmon fly has drawn a fish. I have had fifty-fish days down there. Most are small, wild trout, but I've caught some decent browns too, as much as sixteen inches in length, hook-jawed and feral as a wild horse out on the Wyoming desert.

I go with a four-weight rod, a light, dancing instrument that telegraphs the story of the river to my forearm. I can cast just long enough to cover most of the pools in The Canyon and it is short enough to maneuver over boulders, around trees and through tight passages.

In higher water, it's tough wading in The Canyon. I've inched my way along many a rock face using every climbing technique I know, finger-jamming and toe-jamming, but with my fly rod stuck between my teeth like some mad pirate's blade. It's a trick in wet slippery wading sandals, but around the corner awaits another pool, another slick of water behind a log jam. The price I would pay for a slip and a fall I do not think about. There are hazards, but there are trout to be caught.

There are other dangers there too. A whirring, buzzing rattlesnake once stopped me mid-stride over a clump of sagebrush. I was intent on a big brown I could see finning in the pool and the roar of the water all but muffled Mr. Snake's warning. When my heart sank back down to where it was supposed to be, I eased the foot very slowly back from above the snake, then I backtracked and found another way to angle a cast to the trout.

One year, The Canyon burned, a fire sparked by lightning. It took thousands of acres, pushed by strong winds from the west. It burned down through the gully where my dim trail takes off, and charred both sides of the stream, taking every green thing. In town, I could see the smoke rising over the mountain and I thought about those pools of trout and burning trees all around. That summer, I skipped my trip there, but the next summer, I was back, skeptical. Would where be any fish in the canyon, or had they all been boiled by the fire? I scrambled down the black ash, worked my way through thousands of young aspen sprouting where before there had only been a dark Douglas fir hillside. New brush and wildflowers were everywhere, a green carpet poking up into ash. Life. And at the river, the fishing? Tremendous. It was as if the fishing got better, not worse, after the fire. And so the annual trips continued to my canyon.

Occasionally, I lie on my back and watch the clouds trace their way across the thin mouth of The Canyon. I watch hawks sail in the tricky currents and way up much higher, a jet stream tracks across the sky, reminding me that we can fly too. Sort of.

Late in the day, when the last rays of the sun pass the rim of The Canyon, you shoulder your pack, stow the fly rod and press up the hill, groaning with the grade, resting, scrabbling uphill, slipping, hearing your heart drum in your ears.

At dark, you emerge, muddy, bloody and tired. But never fishless. Ahh, fly fishing!

The Morning Road

Promise is the morning road. The promise of thick trout netted and released. The promise that the new midge pattern you tied last night might entice a fish to strike. The promise of a good day spent in warm sun with a suitable companion. But for now, promise is the road and nothing but the road.

It reaches before you, miles of lonely asphalt over lone prairie and you sip your coffee—spiked heavily with cream—and watch the world around you. Already the day has been a full success, for as you pulled down out of the pines near home, you passed a flock of wild turkeys, the gobbler in late full strut, looking for ladies, feeling the morning. That made not only your morning, but also your day.

What little traffic there is at this early hour in town falls away, and as the town itself dims in the rearview, so too does the traffic. Now, there is only the open road. You pass a school bus, a yellow long box whose cavernous interior has only one student, sitting far in the back as if the driver, a football-field length away, might be carrying something highly contagious. For an hour, this is the only other vehicle you see, but then a '70s era Ford passes you going the other way and the big-hatted driver flicks a two-fingered wave in your direction and you belatedly throw up your own wave in response. It's a flatbed truck and a brindle collie stands balanced perfectly in the middle of the bed, nose to the cool morning wind, drinking it in. Lucky dog.

You see a half dozen other pickups and then a Subaru with mountain bikes atop, but little else. Mostly it is road and wildlife and big open country.

For a while, you thumb through various CDs, trying to find one to fit the mood of the morning road. Ian Tyson singing about leaving Cheyenne and going to Montana seems to work for a while, but then even he gets old, so you shut off the radio, roll down the windows and listen to Wyoming. Most of her song is meadowlarks and bobolinks, but as you slow to enter a tired little town before stomping on the gas pedal again, you hear a pair of sandhill cranes croaking to the morning and later on, killdeer as you pass a prairie pothole.

Antelope stand out brilliant, almost iridescent, in the morning sun and there's a green to the country that you know will last only a few weeks, maybe even a few days in this drought. A kestrel flutters in place and rides the wind and far up, high and away, there's a turkey vulture turning slow circles in brilliant blue.

You hit clouds of bugs too. Mostly midges and gnats and a few thin young mayflies and when you go through them, you wonder if there will be a hatch on the river. But mostly, you just drive and you look out at the morning road.

This is the Wyoming you know and you think about other morning roads, leading other places, but still across Wyoming. Or at least the Wyoming you love the most. Route 191 out of Rock Springs used to be like this one, bare of traffic, jammed with wildlife and fresh cool scenery. You remember a time when those Wyoming roads like 191 and 14-16 out of Ucross were open and empty, not roads of high volume and higher speed. You drive for a while thinking sad-bad thoughts of a time when trucks were all ranch flat beds and brindle collies instead of Oklahoma- and Texas-plated mud-splattered vehicles bearing down at great speed on your bumper and then blurring past en route to big money deep beneath the land. It's dangerous to be a sage grouse or a badger or an antelope or an aficionado of open Wyoming road on some of these highways these days and those thoughts draw you away from the brilliant beauty that is before you. After a while, you pull yourself out of your fret and back to the road and its meadowlarks. You can spend too much time fretting these days, too much time worrying about what is happening out there on the land, happening to that place where you used to hunt antelope, or ride that black stud horse over open country. Too much time thinking and not enough time doing.

Two hours slip away and you wonder about the sanity and the efficiency of driving two hours each way just to catch a few trout that you will let go anyway. And you even think of the hypocrisy in that action, of burning fuel and lamenting the loss of the Wyoming you know in the same breath. It's all about balance, though, for your vehicle gets 50 miles to the gallon and your heart needs the open road. It's all about balance and needing a place where you can drive the morning road and listen to Wyoming's song. There's still that place out there, still that promise of the open road, of what we have and have not lost.

Yet.

The Zone
(or, What I Learned from My Dog)

My first bird dog was a black and white mutt named JD. She was born in a dirt tunnel under a house in Carbondale, Colorado, the year I dropped out of college to fish the Frying Pan, bus tables for the rich and famous, and ski moguls in Aspen. She was the bastard daughter of a springer mother and a rogue black lab, black and white just like the label on a Jack Daniel's bottle. Hence the name. And she was one hell of a dog.

Besides her ability to muscle herself over the vertical sides of a swimming pool fetching tennis balls using agility and brute strength, she was a pretty darned good bird dog. In the pheasant fields, you'd trot along behind her, following her this way and that until her tail started to wag fiercely, her nose pinned to the ground, and you'd know: she's in the Zone. Get ready. Up would go a bird.

Later, I upgraded to real bird dogs, setters, big charging males and delicate females, genuine bird finders. The kind of bird dogs that are born to it. I hunted them into all kinds of wind after all kinds of upland birds from pheasants in the tall grass of South Dakota, to Mearns quail in the oak savannah of southeastern Arizona. They'd ride the breeze like a sailboat, nose up, pulled into it, quartering back and forth and then, suddenly, spinning, following a line of air in one direction. Almost as if tugged by the nose right to the bird. Zeroing in. In the Zone. When this happened, you knew you had better get ready. There would be birds. They didn't make mistakes.

Humans, I believe, have this ability too—but it only comes with time. Lots of time. It's something that is at once primal and surreal, as if you are tapping back to a time when your people etched the images of mammoths and spears onto cave walls. The Zone.

Once, on a wind-swept high plateau in the Wind River Range of Wyoming, I hunted elk with two tags in my pocket. The game managers were trying to keep the elk population down and the bighorn sheep population up in this place, so I figured I'd help. I hunted all afternoon without seeing so much as a track, moving between clumps of limber pine, over a treeless flat. Finally, as the sun tilted west, I prepared to head back to camp, thinking about a hot meal and a cold beer. But there was one small escarpment of rock and pine just ahead of me and for some reason, I thought: I need to look over that little crag. So I climbed up slowly and carefully, drawn by something without knowing it. There, on the lee side of the rock pile, was a small herd of elk, cows and one good bull. I was shooting a single-shot Browning, a reproduction of the old high wall rifles of the late 1800s. I put the crosshairs on the neck of one cow, and broke it. The herd milled at the shot, confused, and I reloaded and shot another cow through the heart. The Zone.

The Zone is an intersection of timing, ability and instinct. You are there or you are not. It is that simple. It can happen at any time and it is something that is neither learned nor forced. It comes from the gut. It happens in the shotgun fields of autumn when every shouldered gun swings perfectly and every shot patterns beautifully. It happens in the dark Doug fir when you step carefully and lightly and follow the scent of elk into an other-worldly intersection of man and quarry. And it happens to me in fishing more than anything.

There will always be times when you are off-kilter, when you stumble around, make bad casts, get distracted by bugs or hot sun or splashing fish or your buddy catching and you not. But when you are in the Zone, it is as if nothing else is in the world except your pin-point precision and concentration.

Not long ago, I fished in the Wyoming Range south of Jackson, Wyoming. I was after fluvial Bonneville cutthroats, big bruising fish that swim up from frog water in the flats of Utah to the clear headwaters of Wyoming. They run seventy miles, many of them. They run through thin dismal waters pulled low and warm to irrigate alfalfa and grass to feed cows. They run past diversions and up creeks you can jump across without getting wet. They sail over beaver ponds that were not there the year before, and scar their backs and bellies on willow sharpened by beaver tooth.

And they are big.

The stream where I was fishing was high and well-muscled, but clear. In the thick current, the big fish were hugging tight against the bank where they might get a foot or less of slack water to feed and hang in. If you were going to catch anything at all in this kind of water, you had to put that fly into a spot about four inches from the bank or closer, mend quickly and often—even mid-cast and mid-air in some cases—and let the fly drift about two feet. You'd have about three attempts to get it right and then the fish would either spook out, or just refuse you. Even more difficult, you could see the fish coming and the strike was neither hard, nor fast. It was subtle and slow and it was all you could do to not yank the fly out of the trout's mouth.

I worked at it most of the day. Sometimes, I'd cast not close enough, out of the feeding lane. Sometimes, I'd stick the fly up on the bank, or snag it on an overhanging damn willow. Sometimes, the current would catch my line before I could mend it and drag the fly right out of the trout's mouth.

But then, I saw a big Bonneville in a spot about three inches wide and eighteen inches long. He was filling most of that space. There weren't any willows nearby, just a bend in the river and a rock to form the slack water for the fish to hold. I estimated the amount of line, made two false casts, landed the fly, mended, mended, and he rose slowly. I saw white as his mouth opened, waited until I didn't see white again, and lifted the hook into him. He was on.

I fought him into the strong current of the main, working him downstream, into a slower eddy, fighting hard now and the fish swimming strong. It lasted for a while, and I held my rod tip high and fed line to him when he wanted it. Softly, he came to the net and I admired him, released him.

I worked upstream, casting better now, confident, landing big flies right tight. I caught more fish, somehow slowing down and concentrating. Now, at last, I was there. The Zone.

We Grow Old
Because We Stop Hiking

July in the Winds. High clouds march like ships across a blue sky. Grasshoppers hover and dance, accompanied by a song that sounds like a thousand back-turning ratchets. The wildflowers have hit their prime and are fading—wrinkled elephanthead in the meadows, fireweed going to seed in the woods, purple monkeyflower clinging stubbornly to the very last of the snowmelt.

It is a time of summer at its midlife, still going strong, yet showing signs of age. In this country, summer's life span is measured in weeks, precious days of full sun and strong light. In many places, even in the high country, the streams are low and warm, and the lakes recede back from the sandy shores, opening sandbars and gravel beds.

The fish seem to know that late July in the tall country means approaching autumn, and I cast again toward the middle of the lake where I can see an underwater shelf that is white as bone and falls off into dark, deep blue. The trout are just beyond the rib of rock, massed where an inlet stream brings a wash of food.

I am working an olive Woolly Bugger, and I strip it toward the bank in long, swift jerks. Out of the depth, a trout rises and strikes, hitting the fly hard enough to startle me a bit, and I raise supple graphite into fish tooth and jaw. The fight takes a few long minutes and I can feel, and then see, the trout shaking its head like a shepherd pup shakes a sock toy. Soon the fish is at hand, a brook trout. A big brook trout, full-chested and colored as only a brook trout is colored, full of fall spawn and finery. I measure it against my fly rod, remembering the length between ferrules. This is no stunted sardine. It's every bit of nineteen inches, a brook trout unlike any I've ever caught. I let him go and he flicks off into the depth and I cast again. I catch four fish that day, all brook trout. The smallest is eighteen inches.

The next day, I am on another lake, still in the southern Winds, still casting for trout. This time, I am waist deep on a long flat, casting to submerged stream channels, double-hauling, giving the five weight every bit of what I've got. I catch four fish. None are smaller than sixteen inches and two are over twenty. They are Yellowstone cutthroats, native to country much farther north but now firmly anchored in this lake and others like it throughout the range.

Few mountain ranges in the world offer the outdoorsman as much as Wyoming's Wind River Range. Miles of trail to ride or backpack, glaciers to climb, some of the world's best granite for rock climbing. And fishing. A map of the Winds tells it—high lakes everywhere, like a fist-full of sapphires thrown lavishly onto a blanket by the Creator. World-famous, well-known fishing. Even today, after so much as been said of the range, the Winds stand as tops for backcountry trout fishing. But it wasn't always this way.

Trout are newcomers to the Winds. One hundred years ago, almost all of the lakes and most of the streams were barren, a trout sink. Waterfalls prevented upstream migration like that of the Colorado River cutthroat on the range's steep western flank, and Yellowstone cutthroat on the more gentle eastern slope. The spine of the continent runs its length, watersheds dropping west and then south to the Colorado River, or east and then north to the Bighorn and then the Yellowstone. This is a place, north to south, east to west, that is rugged, hard, tough to climb into. It's a piece of land that is hard on horseshoes and booted tender toes alike. To travel into the Winds requires sweat equity and stubborn resolve. The rewards, though, make it worth the effort. Fishing is part of that hard-earned bounty. But in order for trout to live in such country, to get a foothold, or more aptly, a fin-hold, they needed a little boost. A boost up over the waterfalls and into the alpine high country.

The man who did the boosting was Finis Mitchell. Finis, which rhymes with highness, was to the Winds and to fishing what Paul Petzoldt was to the Winds and mountain climbing. Both men were sons of pioneer families and both men's hearts were captured by the wild and rugged Wind River Range. Petzoldt founded the world-renowned National Outdoor Leadership School; Mitchell became the hero of every fisherman who ever tied the laces on a pair of hiking boots and then hooked into a trout in the range, including me. That number may now be in the millions.

Mitchell showed up in western Wyoming in 1906 when he was five. Even then, those mountains had a pull on him, and he remembered their snowy flanks during the long wagon trek from Rock Springs north to the family's new homestead on the New Fork. The family had traded forty acres of good Missouri farm ground for one hundred sixty acres of Wyoming sagebrush and sand. Sight unseen. They loaded all of their possessions and farm animals into a railroad boxcar, and when they disembarked at Rock Springs, there was no going back. The Mitchells, just as many Westerners still do today, did what they could to survive. They hauled freight, ran some cattle, raised some hay, got by.

In the Teens, the family finally gave up on the ranch and moved to Rock Springs, but by the time of the Great Depression, the Winds had pulled Finis back. Finis, who was laid off in 1930 from his railroad job, remembered his first thought: "Go to the mountains."

This time, he was married, and he and his wife, Emma, started what they called their fish camp at Big Sandy Opening on the southern tip of the range, where the wild granite and lodgepole falls off into an open wide sagebrush sea. From there, they set up a wall tent, borrowed ten head of horses, and ran dude trips into the mountains. But the fishing wasn't very good. Only a handful of lakes had any fish and these were native cutthroats. So the Mitchells started a stocking program of sorts. They'd catch some fish at one lake, load them up into some cans, and pack them up to a lake that didn't have any fish. At some point, the Wyoming Game and Fish Department got wind of what they were doing in the mountains. Finis remembered the fisheries superintendent coming to him and asking him to stock additional lakes.

"He said, 'We'll bring you the fish if you pack them in free,' and we were tickled to death to get them," said Finis.

Finis loaded up each of six packhorses with two milk cans brimming with water. The cans were loaded with fingerling game fish and covered by burlap. The horsepackers kept the horses moving almost constantly so the water would churn and work oxygen down to the young fish. During the rough trek up into the range, some water sloshed out and the packers—often Finis and his father or brother—refilled them at mountain stream crossings.

By Finis's own count, 314 lakes, mostly in the southwestern part of the range, were stocked in this manner by the Mitchell family and others. In all, he estimated two-and-a-half million fingerling brown, brook, rainbow, golden and cutthroat trout went into these high mountain lakes.

Many of the virgin lakes of the Winds were rich in aquatic insect life, especially those below timberline. The fish grew quickly. Some species reproduced rapidly, a little too rapidly. Brook trout, which are voracious breeders and essentially the English sparrow of the Wind's game fish, took over many lakes. With the benefit of hindsight in 1989, Finis quipped that "it was a very bad mistake," to stock brook trout. "They multiplied and run out of food."

Anyone who has ever fished the typical Wind River brook trout lake or river can attest to the number of small fish and the rarity of big fish. But for the most part, the stocking was a success. Finis told of stocking rainbow trout in Fish Creek Lake and after the fourth year, they were between six and eight pounds. Finis also continued to improvise. One year, he and his father rode over Hailey Pass to Grave Lake, where they caught several lake trout that they packed back over the pass and stocked in Mae's Lake, which Finis had named for his daughter.

Throughout most of the decade of the 1930s, the fishing camp provided enough money for the Mitchells to get by, but a steady job became available toward the beginning of World War II, and Finis hired back on with the railroad and moved back to Rock Springs. But the mountains never left him; in fact, they tightened their grip on his being. Now, he could work four long shifts and have three days off every week. Every spare moment was mountain time. He explored the Winds from top to bottom, and took up photography, shooting thousands of slides of the Winds, its wildlife, and wonders. He made it widely known that he wanted to explore every corner of the Winds, and during his long life, it's likely that he came as close to doing that as any person before or since.

Finis practically invented the "go light" philosophy that is the mantra of today's backpacker. In fact, he took it to a high art. His gear consisted of a tarp, a sleeping bag, cheap boots and an inexpensive pack frame. He cooked nothing, eating only dried foods, Emma's special high-octane fruitcake, and cheese. He drank right out of the streams and wore bib overalls almost all the time; every picture you see of him displays this fashion taste.

In late August 1960, Finis was caught above timberline in a fierce snowstorm that lasted three days. Rather than panic, he hunkered down and waited out the storm, covering himself up with his sleeping bag and resting under a blanket of snow. Nearby, a band of wild sheep kept him company. "They fed all around me," he told *Audubon* magazine in 1985. "We shared a waterhole. I learned more about bighorns than I had in all my life before."

The man was obviously a survivor and his knowledge of the Winds grew with each trip. His vacations and nearly every summer weekend were spent in the Winds. He often traveled alone, with his longest solo expedition lasting seventeen days.

While anti-wilderness enthusiasts contend that wilderness preservation is the gone-awry privilege of Eastern white-collar intellectuals, Finis—raised on Wyoming's sagebrush flats in the shadow of the Winds before the emergence of the automobile, never educated beyond the eighth grade, and blue-collar railroader to the core—was a die-hard wilderness advocate. Consider: "We must strive to preserve this wilderness for innocent souls yet to follow in our footsteps; that they, too, may enjoy a wilderness with all its bounties, and learn to preserve it for those to follow them."

And: "Man's very existance [sic] lies with the earth. That is why our wilderness areas have been set aside, to keep them from exploiting all the earth. At every opportunity any area that qualifies should be added to it and preserved for coming generations."

Finis wrote those words, and many more, in a little book that has become a classic, *Wind River Trails*. Published in 1975, the book—as if patterned after Mitchell's own minimalist philosophy—is small and light enough to go into the pocket of a backpack and head up the mountain with its owner. It's part guidebook, part fishing book, part philosophy. It is the result of all that slogging up mountain trails, climbing mountain passes and peaks, camping out under the stars, and heading off to yet another unexplored drainage.

The author's note in the front of *Trails* offers this short resume: "A short hike…years ago was the beginning of a long career in wilderness living for Finis Mitchell …He has scaled 244 peaks, including four times to the top of Gannett Peak, the highest mountain in the state. A vigorous supporter of wilderness, the mountain man pours out his philosophy at meetings and slide shows with amazing attention to detail. He has taken 105,345 pictures as a hobby and uses them in his slide shows to show people their own public lands."

By the time Finis had quit taking photographs, that number was closer to 120,000. *Wind River Trails* went through numerous printings and Mitchell, always the advocate of wilderness and the range itself, was recognized for his devotion. The U.S. Geological Survey sent him maps of the range to proofread and fact-check before they were printed. Finis was featured in numerous magazines and newspapers and was given an honorary doctorate from the University of Wyoming. Even more impressive, Finis had a peak named in his honor, 12,482-foot Mitchell Peak, located in the southern Winds just east and a little south of the famed Cirque of the Towers. He climbed it at least eighteen times. He also served in the Wyoming House of Representatives from 1955 to 1958. But despite all of the accolades and accomplishments, Finis was still mountain to the core.

Even late in his life—indeed *Wind River Trails* was published when he was seventy-four—Mitchell kept going to the mountains, sticking to his oft-quoted philosophy: "We don't stop hiking because we grow old, we grow old because we stop hiking."

But when he was seventy-three, he took a bad fall in a crevasse on a glacier. He badly twisted his knee and couldn't walk, so he crawled out, made an ice pack by cutting up his long underwear and waited two days for the swelling to go down. Meanwhile, he whittled some crutches and then when he could move, he hobbled eighteen miles out of the wilderness. Later, a stroke slowed him. Even so, he would often lead trips up onto what he called his "Sacred Rim," at the edge of Fremont Gorge with stunning views of the high Winds. As his physical ability dwindled, he used walking sticks in each hand. He was determined not to stop hiking, but on November 13, 1995, he finally did, passing away just one day shy of his ninety-fourth birthday.

Not long before Mitchell's death, my friend Walt Gasson, a son of Green River, Wyoming, happened to be in that town visiting a relative in a nursing home. While walking down the hall headed out, he saw a nameplate on a door that make him stop in his tracks. It read: Finis Mitchell. Gasson peered in through the open door and saw Finis lying on his back, pale, shrunken, staring blankly at the ceiling.

Shaking his head sadly, Gasson told that story to me and *Wyoming Wildlife* editor Chris Madson one day. "If ever a guy should have been out on some talus slope somewhere at 13,000 feet..."

"He probably was," said Madson.

Gold

It is late summer and above us stands a massive granite wall so typical of this range. We will climb that wall tomorrow, but today is a day of rest. There are a dozen of us, all honed thin by weeks in the mountains, weeks scrambling over boulders, climbing across glaciers, going up and then down mountain passes and peaks. The days have fallen behind us like spring cottonwood fluff thrown into the wind, but each passing day brings a new memory.

This one, this fine day of high thin blue sky is a day of fishing. For nearly two weeks, we've been above the fish, right on the very spine of the range, scrambling in nosebleed country. Today, though, we will drop.

Below us, perhaps one thousand feet, is a stream that looks as if made by the hand of a mighty fly fisherman. Deep pools. Riffles. Boulders. Willow and spruce line its banks and we scramble down to them and cast. For an hour, we flog the water, throwing anything and everything until finally it dawns upon us that the water is undimpled by feeding trout, unfinned by swimming fish. Surely a stream this beautiful cannot be empty? But it is, and as we follow it on its journey downstream toward the Big Horn, we find out why. A waterfall.

Below it, we start to catch trout. They are small, but large enough to eat, and we are hungry. Catch-and-release becomes a fairy tale when your belly has been filled for two weeks with six varieties of pasta, trail mix, and pancakes spiced different ways every morning. Meat! Give us protein!

The first trout brings us the joy of consumption but also something else. Not only is he unusual for living so high in the mountains, but it is his hide that snares our breath. Vivid gold and red paints his belly and a cherry-red stripe runs the length of his side. Above he is green and his tail is peppered in black. He is a golden trout. Quite literally. He is, at least to our non-fisheries-biologist eyes, genetically pure.

In the world of fish and fishing, no other trout defines places above timberline, places swept clean from the fingerprints of man, places of fragile beauty and rare oxygen, than does the golden trout. It is a fish that does best where man is not, a trout that refuses to be propagated in hatcheries, a fish that swims only the purest water.

For eons, that water was found in a small drainage in California's southern Sierra Nevada. In a small portion of the range drained by the Kern River, the golden trout evolved. Biologists speculate that the golden trout is descended from rainbow trout that made their way up the rivers and then were geographically isolated, evolving over thousands of years into a separate species. Whatever the cause, there can be no doubt that the golden trout is unique. No other trout species on the continent makes quite the splash that he does.

In the 1800s, he was "discovered" by white men who came into the area looking for gold and found the golden. Beautiful, abundant, and tasty, the trout almost became yet another victim of that bloodthirsty era. Early accounts recall men catching and wasting as many as 400 golden trout in a day. It was a formula primed for disaster: an isolated population of a unique species that lived nowhere else in the world discovered in an era where excess in hunting and fishing was the norm. Moreover, the fishing was unregulated.

But there were a few men who saw the fish for what it was. One was a novelist and a conservationist, the other was an entrepreneur and Civil War veteran.

The novelist was Stewart Edward White, author of fiction and nonfiction books often set in the High Sierra. White was a hunter, a fisherman, and above all, a conservationist. In the golden trout, he saw something very special: "I can liken it to nothing more accurately than the twenty-dollar gold piece, the same satin finish, the same pale yellow. The fish was fairly molten. It did not glitter in gaudy burnishment, as does our aquarium goldfish, for example, but gleamed and melted and glowed as though fresh from the mold...Furthermore, along either side of the belly ran two broad longitudinal stripes of exactly the color and burnish of the copper paint used on racing yachts. I thought then, and have ever since, that the Golden Trout, fresh from the water, is one of the most beautiful fish that swims."

Early on, White noted his concern for the golden trout's survival. "Well-meaning people used to laugh at the idea that the buffalo and wild pigeons would ever disappear. They are gone...As the certainly increasing tide of summer immigration gains in volume, the Golden Trout, in spite of his extraordinary numbers at present, is going to be caught out.

"Therefore, it seems the manifest duty of the Fisheries to provide for the proper protection and distribution of this species, especially the distribution. Hundreds of streams in the Sierras are without trout simply because of some natural obstruction, such as a waterfall too high to jump, which prevents their ascent of the current. These are well adapted to the planting of fish and might just as well be stocked by the Golden Trout as the customary Rainbow."

White had friends in high places. The highest place, in fact. He hit up his old buddy, Theodore Roosevelt, for some help in protecting the golden. Roosevelt put his commissioner of fisheries onto the problem and a protection plan that included stocking barren lakes in the Sierra was enacted. In honor of White's efforts, the Little Kern golden trout was dubbed *Salmo whitei* in 1906.

But even before White entered the picture, a stocking program of sorts had already been undertaken. In the 1870s, a Civil War veteran, Colonel Sherman Stevens, built a sawmill on Cottonwood Creek, not far from the Kern River drainage where golden trout thrived. But, as with many streams of that era, not a single trout swam the waters of Cottonwood Creek. So in 1876, Stevens packed twelve fish in a coffee pot from Mulkey Creek on the Kern drainage over into Cottonwood. While Stevens' motivations may not have been as pure as White's— Stevens wanted to be able to have trout to feed the men who worked the sawmill—the results were impressive. Cottonwood Creek proved to be ideal habitat for the golden trout and they thrived. A decade or two later, goldens had moved farther up the drainage and had even been placed into Cottonwood Lakes and the head of the drainage. Cottonwood Lakes became the nucleus of the golden trout stocking program enacted by the California Department of Fish and Game and aggressively pursued in and out of state.

This program continued for several years until 1939 when the California Legislature banned exportation of golden trout eggs in a move that Phil Pister, a retired fisheries biologist with the state, calls "a classic example of political stupidity." Nevertheless, the ban lasted for several decades and was lifted only in recent years. Fortunately for anglers elsewhere, like Wyoming, golden trout came east before the ban.

High mountains. Clear streams. Pristine lakes fed by snowmelt and glaciers. Far-back country seldom visited by humans. These are the ingredients in the recipe for healthy golden trout populations. California's Sierra Nevada has them. So does Wyoming. And Montana. And Idaho. Colorado. When California launched its program to stock goldens outside the Kern River drainage, outside the state, these states all got on the list. Wyoming, especially the Wind River Range, became the epicenter of golden trout in a new age.

Legend has it that the first goldens to come to Wyoming were actually headed for some eastern state. But when the train carrying the live cargo stopped in southwestern Wyoming, inspectors found that the trout were dying. They made a hurried decision to stock the fish into Cook Lake high in the Wind River Mountains near Pinedale. It's a romantic vision—I picture trout packed in milk cans filled with clean Sierra water, and officials scrambling to load them into Model A trucks, then driving north from Green River on a road that was little more than a trail. At the end of the line—probably Pinedale—the milk cans are packed onto reluctant mules and head into the high country. A true tale? Perhaps. But if the trout were dying in Green River, how did they survive the trip north over miles of bad road, and then mule-back into the tallest country in the state?

Regardless, somehow Cook Lake got some golden trout. The result was impressive because Cook was devoid of fish, yet rich in fish food. What the lake churned out after being stocked was big fish and lots of them. The world's record golden trout is an eleven-pounder yanked from Cook Lake in the 1950s.

While fables are interesting, what is known for certain is that golden trout were stocked in Wyoming's waters in 1929. Today, 123 lakes in the state's high mountain ranges have golden trout populations. Almost all of these waters are in the Wind River, Beartooth, and Bighorn mountain ranges—ranges not too unlike their native Sierra.

Golden trout in Wyoming are very popular among a robust smattering of fishermen tough enough to climb the tall country in search of a unique fish. For years, Wyoming, perhaps even more so than homeland California, has been the place to go if an angler wanted to catch a golden trout.

The non-native fish found Wyoming's cold high lakes to be virtually identical to their home waters and they flourished. Wyoming Game and Fish Department personnel helped them along. For several decades, Cook Lake became the repository of golden trout for the state. Unlike the popular brown, rainbow, and even cutthroat trout, golden trout steadfastly refuse to be propagated in low-country hatcheries.

"Goldens are the most difficult we've ever seen," says Steve Sharon, a fisheries biologist for Wyoming. "We've tried on numerous occasions to get them to spawn in a hatchery, but the timing is off because sometimes the males will be ready and the females won't and the other way around. Elevation does play a key role."

The result is that biologists had to collect golden trout eggs the old-fashioned way, by packing into the high mountain lakes in the spring and spawning the fish out there. The fertilized eggs were then taken to a hatchery where they were grown into little fish in the three-inch range. These fish were then stocked into other waters around the state.

But in 1954, Cook Lake was abandoned as a brood stock lake in favor of Surprise Lake on Fall Creek in the Winds. Sadly, Cook Lake's golden trout fishery collapsed when aggressive brook trout got into the lakes. Brookies, though not able to interbreed with golden trout, are able to reproduce in large numbers and out-compete goldens for food.

Surprise Lake became the nucleus of the department's golden trout brood stock, producing eggs for Wyoming waters each year; between 25,000 and 40,000 tiny golden trout were planted in high mountain lakes each year between 1955 and 1993. But in 1988, the same year that fires swept through Yellowstone, a forest fire known as the Fayette Fire dramatically altered the terrain at Surprise Lake, burning the spruce and fir canopy. For several years after the fire, large amounts of debris and sediment went into the lake from the burn during spring runoff. Eventually, the productivity of the lake declined, and Surprise Lake was abandoned as a golden trout brood stock lake.

Consequently, for more than a decade, Wyoming has not planted golden trout anywhere. But perhaps fisheries biologists will be able to turn that around.

Ever since the loss of the brood stock in Surprise Lake, Wyoming scientists have been talking to fisheries biologists in the California Fish and Game Department about getting golden trout.

Then there's the other side of the hill from Pinedale—the Wind River Indian Reservation. Remote, with few maintained trails, and lots of high mountain lakes and streams, the "Rez" is a place of wild country set on edge. It has some of the best golden trout habitat in the world in its wilderness backcountry and the U.S. Fish and Wildlife Service has been working with the two tribes that call the Rez home, the Shoshone and Arapaho. The tribes have been in turn working with the state biologists.

Some half dozen lakes in several mountain ranges and on the reservation have been identified as ideal brood stock lakes. Currently, these lakes are barren, yet they have good outlet or inlet streams and good pea-sized gravel for spawning.

"We want to learn from our mistake at Surprise Lake—we don't want to put all of our eggs in one basket," says Sharon. "The goal is to be able to spawn a minimum of 100 pairs of goldens every year. We want to develop the program right and develop populations that we can maintain through stocking and possible natural reproduction."

Many of the lakes that have been planted with goldens in the past do not have natural reproduction. As the trout age and are caught by anglers, the lake has fewer and fewer fish until they are eventually gone. As the stocking program has languished, a few lakes have lost their golden trout populations altogether. A couple of lakes in the Snowy Range outside Laramie that once had goldens are now being stocked with other species.

Yet for now, it appears as if most of the self-sustaining populations in the state are holding their own.

"What we are trying to do is reestablish our brood stock, working with the reservation, and looking to establish some populations there as well," says Sharon. "We can build some repositories for California and also some genetic backups for the state of Wyoming. Given the history of the golden trout, it's important to get them up here and protect them."

Protecting rare and unusual fish has been the life work of Phil Pister of the Desert Fishes Council. Pister retired from the California Department of Fish and Game in 1990 after a career that spanned nearly four decades. He spent much of his time trying to protect the golden trout in its native habitat.

In the 1960s, Pister heard reports of brown trout being caught in the Kern River drainage in prime golden trout habitat. Brown trout, while a very popular game fish, are voracious predators. They found the Kern to their liking. In 1969, Pister went up to the South Fork of the Kern with a fish shocker.

"We hadn't even gone fifteen feet when we put a five-pound brown out from under the bank," remembers Pister.

For the better part of the next thirty years, California fisheries biologists were in high gear trying to eradicate brown and other exotic fish from the Kern and its tributaries. "We basically rotenoned everything that was wet," says Pister.

Rotenone is a chemical commonly used to treat streams that have undesirable fish. The chemical basically shuts off the oxygen supply for the fish and they die. Prior to treating the streams, the biologists captured the goldens and then restocked them after the streams were clear.

"It was a major effort to get rid of the browns before they could just eat the goldens," says Pister. "But the golden is California's state fish, so it was really no problem to get money from the legislature to protect them."

Workers also built fish barriers to keep the browns from coming back up the river to the treated areas. Some of the barriers were massive, such as the one made out of eighty cubic yards of concrete that had to be flown in by helicopter.

Other exotics such as rainbow trout pose a different set of problems to goldens, and to California's repository of them, Cottonwood Lake. Several biologists, including Pister, believe that Cottonwood Lake trout are genetically impure and have actually interbred with rainbow trout.

"We've been fooling ourselves. They are not pure goldens; they've got rainbow genes," says Pister.

California is examining the genetics of its brood stock and is also looking at other places in the drainage where there are pure golden trout. Even if the Cottonwood Lakes trout are pure goldens, their genetic integrity might be compromised because these are the fish that were started from the dozen or so fish that Colonel Stevens stocked into the drainage in the 1800s.

"I think that they are losing vigor and the fitness of the population," says Sharon. "If we are going to develop a program, I think we should do it right for the future of populations two or three hundred years down the road."

In high mountain lakes, where sunlight washes across granite boulder fields just long enough each summer to melt ice that is as thick as the chest of an Angus bull, golden trout swim. They swim in cold, clear alpine water where the only sounds are the occasional jet streaming high overhead, or the bark of a pika from the rubble heap, or the relentless lash of wind on ridgetop.

Wyoming and Montana both have pure golden trout and both are working to preserve—and even expand—this shining trout in high lakes. If you are tough enough, determined to climb long trails shaded by lodgepole pine, to climb higher and higher to krummholz country, and on up into the tall places of forever snow, then you will find them there, against the crest of the world.

And so it is. The summer rolls onward and our crew backpacks from high mountain hold to another windswept mountain hold. Early one morning, we top and rise above a lake that stands far above timberline. A crag of granite rises from its east end and the water is dead calm and pure, reflecting the unrippled image of the crag. At the inlet, though, things are happening.

Trout. I drop my pack at my feet, sweating hard, and pull a pair of polarized sunglasses on. At the head of the lake is a large school of feeding fish. I can see them there, spinning in the water, moving here and there, flashing white as mouths open to feed, rising and dropping and chasing one another. I look to my hiking friend: "I need a minute."

I joint together my pack rod, all five pieces, trembling. I can see a light hatch of midges and I thumb through my fly box. I am traveling light and I find a size 22 black gnat. The fish look as if they are taking just below the surface, for they porpoise, big dorsal fins breaking the water's edge. I cast, a long tight loop that lands splashless and I fish the gnat wet, making a slow retrieve until I feel a heaviness on the line and I lift the rod tip into it.

The fish fights hard, strong muscle pulling line out of my fingers, taking line out into the depths of the lake and then back. I work slowly, for the leader is twelve feet and is tipped only by 7X. It is a delicate dance and when I work him closely, I see his sides, golden yellow but "gleamed and melted and glowed as though fresh from the mold."

Beneath an Untracked Sky

There's not much to go by, just a yard light by the corrals. The stars, though there are a lot of them in the clear sky, aren't any help. It doesn't matter much, for the truck is loaded and the horses we are taking are in the corrals already. We've both gulped a quick bowl of cereal and two cups of coffee. Now we are in the corral and the horses are playing with us, running from one end to the other. My ride horse, a pale palomino that reminds me of the first horse I ever owned, is easy to catch.

Her horse, a little buckskin not much bigger than a pony that she bought at the sale barn maybe a week ago, is harder. He dodges and weaves in the corral for a few minutes. In the dark, you can't see his black legs, only the pale hide. It floats legless from one end of the corral to the other. I've caught two of the pack horses while she has been dancing with the buckskin. *Maybe that's why they ran him through the sale,* but I keep that thought down. She is stressing, I can tell by the way her shoulders are stiff under her black wave of hair, by her increasingly quick movements as she tries to pin the little pony-horse into a corner. I don't move to help her. This is a gal who likes to do things on her own. I've learned that in the last two weeks. She's an Italian beauty with the soul of an artist. I best let it happen.

She does catch him in a few minutes, minutes that seemed longer than they were, the stress bunching up in the lady's shoulders and arms, but she finally gets him in a corner. I've got the other pack horses caught and tied to the fence and she moves in on the little horse and pins him, talking softly, sweetly, although I know she's pissed. It's good to remember that. Soft, sweet talk means she's pissed. I make a mental note of it. She's running the show today, I'm just along for the heavy lifting.

It's still dark as we load the horses into the gooseneck, talking softly to the horses, and to each other.

"Okay, bring up Kirby. Okay, now Gambler. That's it, good. Nice boy." She's cooing to the horse, gentle talk.

Working in the dark, lead ropes slung over a cold metal bar inside the trailer. Not tied solid, for if a horse goes down in the bouncing trailer on the way to the trailhead, you want him to be able to scramble up, to get out from under all those hooves, to move. It smells of horse in the trailer, of road dust and dried manure. It is still night when we get them all loaded and I look up toward Orion's Belt as I thumb the door of the passenger side of the quad cab. Orion the Hunter. It's that time now, a hint of coldness in the air, the fresh-snap smell of turning aspens in the air. Not a better time of year in the mountains. She's driving.

My fishing rod is cased behind my saddle, a rod that I can transport almost anywhere and joint together. There's a mountain stream where we are going, a stream that I've ridden past many times, but never fished. I want to fish it today, to watch brook trout come to the fly, to smell that tangy scent of coming autumn on the wind off the mountain. It is the promise of the stream never fished but often desired that drives an angler's soul. I've ridden or walked past this stream—riffles and bends and slack water and bounce-water boulder runs—too many times.

"Okay, we got everything?"

It's a way of making conversation more than anything. I know it's a stupid comment, for we packed it all last night, the pack saddles and riding saddles up in the nose of the gooseneck, the boxes of food in the bed of the pickup, already weighed and placed in the panniers. All we've got to do when we get to the trailhead is sling loads and ride. There's a bunch of hungry kids in the mountains who have been out climbing rocks and learning how to camp in the Wyoming wilderness. They'll be glad to see us.

"We packed it all last night."

It comes off her tongue sharp, but I let it go. It's early yet and I know she's edgy. She's in charge here, for she's been doing this all summer. I'm just along for the ride, for the high country. She grinds the quad cab into granny and we pull out of the yard as gently as a one ton truck and a gooseneck can, crawling over the river rock that is the road on this hardscrabble outfitting ranch, and up to the gate, turning east toward the southern toe of the Wind River Mountains.

Our destination is Big Sandy Opening, "BSO" among the veteran packers. Ten or twelve miles in to the lake and we'll meet the kids and their instructors, greet them with fresh food and letters from back home, pack up their trash and broken equipment, anything they don't need for the next two weeks, then ride back out again. Maybe this time, I'll get a little fishing in.

In the east, the sky is turning a little bit whiter, an edge of blue-black in a black sea. It's so clear out it makes my eyes water. There isn't a cloud anywhere. We bounce the pickup and trailer over a thin-surfaced road, barely more than a single layer of asphalt glued onto an old hard-pack. It's not any smoother than a gravel road, but it is less dusty. When we turn off the pavement, the trip gets rougher and dustier and by the time we get to the trailhead, there's a thin layer of dust over everything, the panniers, the saddles, the horses in the back.

They shake and blow as we take them out of the trailer and tie them up to it and to the hitchracks that the Forest Service has thoughtfully placed here.

By now, the light has come up, that thin pale blue light of pre-dawn, a light that always seems colder than night, a chill that creeps into your core before the sun crests the ridge and hits you warm and full. I'm thinking about bull elk and hungry trout, but the morning buzz is broken by the sound of a radio coming from the backpackers' parking lot. There are two parking lots at BSO, one for the horses and packers, and one for everybody else. We are too busy packing, tightening cinches, clucking to our stock, building and slinging loads, to pay much attention. Not even seven o'clock and some bastard is playing a radio. Radios and mountains don't fit. We look across the back of the horse we are packing and shake our heads in unison.

"Can you believe that?"

"No," I say. "Pretty inconsiderate."

It's not music. News. Someone is blasting out the trailhead with news. The other trailhead, with perhaps six cars parked there on this Indian Summer morning, is about three hundred yards away across a frosted meadow, but the radio is as clear as if it were on the bumper of our pickup. We are too busy to listen to the words and wouldn't anyway if we could take the time. We're in agreement that radios don't fit out here.

"Cinch. Rope. Okay, ready? Rope."

It's the talk of packers at work, and we have all the horses loaded quickly. I can see the stiffness fading a bit from her shoulders and she smiles at me as we work. It's the kind of smile you'd pay good money for.

She walks the little buckskin away from the trailer and tries him out. He stands easy as she swings up and turns him in a circle, backs him. Like all of his nonsense was saved for the dark corral. Maybe she got a buy after all. I hand the lead rope of her short packstring up to her and then swing up onto the palomino, right hand full of lead rope for my own pack string. We skirt through the lodgepole, listening to the soft thump of horse hoof on dusty trail. Somewhere off in the woods, a woodpecker beats his head against a tree. The radio has gone off.

I think about fish again, about the trout stream I've been wanting to try all these years. Somehow, there was always an excuse to keep going: the sun was dropping west and we had to get to camp, it looked like it was going to rain, there weren't any fish rising. And so on. This time, though, there will be enough time to fish and I can feel it up ahead of us, up there in that valley beneath a tall mountain already varnished with the first snow of the season.

There's a man standing in the trail when we round the other parking lot and head up country, up along the river. He's standing solid in the trail, looking at the trailhead sign, at all of the posters there. Maybe, I think, he's signing in. That's something I hardly ever do, especially with a pack string slung out behind me. This guy sees us, but he doesn't move. Instead he turns and looks up at us.

"Were you listening to your radio?"

Oh boy, here it comes, the guy thinks we were the ones playing the radio and he's going to give us grief about it.

"No, we weren't," she says. "Somebody was. We could hear it."

"Our nation is under attack."

You meet all kinds in the mountains. Once I came across a lone, bearded man far back in the Winds, walking along a trail, mumbling to himself. Another time, I met a Boy Scout leader who was packing more fat than pack. He'd fallen behind his boys, far behind, and he sat on a log chain-smoking no-filter Marlboros. All of this wasn't so weird, except this guy was wearing Sorrels, those thick, insulated boots that you wear out feeding in the middle of winter. This was the middle of July.

This guy must be one of those.

"Huh. Well, that's weird," I couldn't think of much else to say. Stupid comments had been pouring out of my mouth most of the morning.

"Yes, the White House is on fire, the Twin Towers have been demolished and someone flew a plane into the Pentagon. It's all over the radio."

We pull our string to a stop and sit for a moment.

The guy's a nut, but I keep that thought under my hat just as I did my thought about the buckskin horse-pony. Then he introduces himself. He's a preacher from Rock Springs. Perhaps a religious nut?

We turn our string to the trail ahead, leaving the man standing in the trail, looking off to the mountains. Maybe he's praying now.

We ride in silence for a while, listening to the string, smelling those good smells of horse and leather, pine and mountain wind, crisp aspen.

"What do you think of that?"

"Can't be real, I mean, the guy is some kind of weirdo, don't you think? I mean, well, I guess it could be true. But I doubt it." Thinking that pretty women make me babble like a fool.

"But he introduced himself, don't you think that's weird?"

She has a point there.

"Well, if it's true and this is the end of the world, we've got enough food here on these horses to just keep on riding right to Canada."

It's a good thought, for ahead is the entire spine of the range, better than one hundred miles, and then Yellowstone and then the Gallatin Range, then a big Montana valley and another range and pretty soon the Bob Marshall and Glacier and eventually, Canada. Riding to Canada with a pack string of sound ponies and a female camping companion. A fishing rod behind my saddle. "When we run out of food, we can survive on trout. There's worse ways to go through the world."

She laughs at that one and the sound is musical and lovely. I know this thing between her and me probably isn't going to last, but it sure feels good right now.

She looks good in the saddle, straight back, long mane of black hair beneath her hat, wearing an old snap-button cotton shirt of mine that never looked that good on me. Wranglers. Women in Wranglers. It's good to know your weak spots. She seems a little less tense than she did this morning. Maybe she's thinking that if it's true, we could ride on into the far reaches of the continent before we'd run out of food. Or maybe she's thinking that if it is true, it doesn't make much sense to stress out over things like horses that are hard to catch and dumb questions from the man she's seeing. Or that if the world is ending, it is better ended on horseback in wild country with a good fly rod tied behind the saddle. Or at least, that's what I'd like to think she's thinking. So I ask her.

"Oh, I'm thinking that if this is the end of the world, there's no place I'd rather be."

The trail climbs though stands of lodgepole, and winds beside meadows of sun-cured grass. In the distance, we can hear the Big Sandy laughing over smooth stone. The sun is on us now, and it feels good. There's been a frost and there are no bugs. Just warm sunshine and horses going up-country into the tall-back.

"Me too."

For two hours, we ride and the conversation swings back and forth. We see no one else, so we can't find out if the preacher was a nut or telling the truth. Even if we did run into someone else, they probably would know less than we would. Cell phones don't work up here and radio signals are few.

It takes this long for the uniqueness of this day to sink into our souls and when it does, it comes with a quick realization. We've been riding to the sound of our stock, the jingle of bit, the snort that clears a dusty nostril, the creak of saddle leather, the chatter of a pine squirrel out in the timber somewhere. But with all of this, it's intensely quiet. There is no background noise, only the sound of man and animal. Even in a wild country like the Wind River Range, you can hear jets passing overhead, a constant hum that remind us that there are other people on this planet and they are going somewhere too.

She says it first. "Have you seen any jet trails in the sky?"

The sky has been drawing my eye all day, but until she says it, I didn't know why. "No, not a one. And you can't hear anything either. There's no sound. You don't think what that guy was saying is true, do you?"

"He had said something about jet traffic being grounded, the commerce of the nation at a dead stop." That comes back to me again as I tilt my hat back and look at the sky. There are no jet contrails, no signs that anyone but us lives on this planet. Even the trail is clean of tracks. No tracks in the sky. No tracks on the ground.

Silence overcomes us now and we just listen to the pack string and ride. All the sounds are natural, even the clink of steel on stone.

I find myself sweeping my eyes again and again at the horizon. It is untracked pure blue, a slate as clean as a meadow of fresh snow.

At the rendezvous point, we pull the packs off the tired horses, leaving them tied in a stand of whitebark pine, swishing tails lazily at non-existent flies. It's fall up here, up high where the grass is the same color as the hide on that buckskin horse, and a tint of yellow splashes the willows along the stream. There's a smell to the place too, and a dusting of new snow up on the granite way high. But that sky, that amazing sky. We can't take our eyes off of it, all of that blue without clouds, without streaks of white telling us a jet went on its way. Now, for really the first time, we begin to admit that perhaps that preacher from Rock Springs wasn't a nut at all, but a person of good intent and honest delivery. Perhaps the world is coming to an end, but even this thought seems as out of place now as that trackless sky. We've been living with a jet-streaked sky all of our lives. We know nothing else. For two modern mountain horsepackers, it is the natural, untracked sky that doesn't fit. But mostly, it is the silence, for there is no sound of engines, no far-off buzz of fuel burning. There is only us and there is only now and that has us leaning back on one arm in the full warmth of the autumn sun looking at the sky and wondering what is next.

By the time the hungry backpackers show up for their food, we've made our minds up that there is truth in the trackless sky. When the first thing out of the mouth of the course leader is to ask us if we've got a radio, we realize it fully. The course was up high where they had radio reception on a shortwave and they had heard it too. Planes flying into tall buildings in New York. The Pentagon burning. Reports of a plane missing over Pennsylvania. Chaos. Death.

It doesn't fit into our world of mountains and horses though. We are lost in thought, but in the moment. So we ride, quiet, leaving the course behind us. Just the two of us now. It seems better that way. Somehow. The world seemed pretty amazing where there was just her and me and a ride beneath a sky without tracks.

It is only when I am back at the truck, unsaddling my ride horse, that I see the fly rod, still in its case, rolled in my rain slicker. It never even occurred to me to fish.

The Quest

I had heard of the river many times before I saw it. The Thorofare. The name sang. It sang to me personally. It sang of people like Roosevelt and Bridger, of men of another time. It sang of wild country and wild creatures. Mostly the river sang of trout, a wild trout as long as a man's shinbone, a trout unchanged for eons. It was called the Yellowstone cutthroat. I had heard stories, read articles, and watched a video where a hot-shot dude horseman caught a big trout from a Thorofare riffle without even stepping out of the saddle. I had to go.

It was the Fourth of July, 1994. We set up camp in the meadows not far from where the Thorofare joins the Yellowstone on the way to the big lake where most of the river trout lived. But in the spring, starting in June and running through July, those big fish came up out of the lake and into the rivers and streams that fed it. We camped for four days. We got snowed on one night, and fought terrific mosquitoes the next. We caught trout, big trout, so long that their tales lipped out over the edge of the fry pan. Most we released, their sides striped in yellow and red, their flanks dotted with black as if they had been splashed with mud from a passing truck. When we left that wild place, memories of trout bending a fly rod, of campfires and laughter stayed in our bones. Those memories will be there when we are old men, for old men remember the days of the young man and the young man always is alive in the old. Always.

Thoughts of that pure cutthroat crept into my soul every year. I started thinking about other natives in other places, places perhaps not as far back into the tall country, but places still wild enough to hold a trout that was pure like his ancestors. Then I heard about the Cutt-Slam. Four subspecies of cutthroat trout in four different waters around the big state of Wyoming. I had my Yellowstone. But there were others other there: the Colorado River, the Bonneville, and the Snake River. And there is only one unique place in the whole world where a person can catch all three—the little-known Wyoming Range.

At the time, I was living on the wrong end of the state for catching pure cutthroat trout. An expedition was in order. It would mean driving miles and miles, and pinching the feat of the three subspecies into one long weekend. Colleagues had caught all four in two days, but to me that seemed like an exercise, not a fishing expedition.

One Friday, four of us piled into my old Dodge diesel, a geriatric beast with 199,600 miles on the odometer. We chased the sinking sun west, then drove in the dark, pounding up a long road to the edge of the Wyoming Range. At the tiny burg of Big Piney, we turned farther west, then found a wide spot in the road and pushed up the pop-up camper and climbed in.

At dawn, we rose and drove to LaBarge Creek, where there were rumors of Colorado River cutthroat. The four of us spread out. Two were amateur fishermen who needed casting and catching lessons—and we spent about thirty minutes with this chore before my friend Janet and I were called to the stream. A competitive woman, Janet is not one to suffer beginners when there are fish to be caught. I'm no better. At the stream, I caught my first Colorado River, a six-inch fish. Janet was below and did not hear me yelling for the camera, so I set off in her direction, found her fishing a long run between willows and aspens, and had her stop long enough to take a picture. Janet set her jaw and fished harder. Finally, she hooked a fish smaller than mine, but a Colorado River nevertheless.

As the day faded, we drove up the long road to the head of LaBarge Creek, past a vast sweep of meadow where pioneers en route to Oregon stopped on the Lander Cuttoff. It was a pristine sweep of land, with the stream snaking through the bottom, a stream that you could jump across without getting a running start. At the head of the meadow, we pushed up and over the tri-basin divide, where the range splits and waters drain to the Columbia, the Great Basin, and the Colorado. We topped the divide and drove down the Greys, watching it grow from a trickle, to a big stream, to a river. We stopped and fished and Janet whooped and had a pure Snake River in her net in minutes. I set my jaw and then caught mine. Pictures were taken. Beers were cracked. Toasts were made.

We spent the day on the river, now with time and patience enough to give fishing lessons and that night we listened to coyotes in the meadow above our camp and thought about the special place we were and about the pleasure of catching pure fish in their native waters. We thought, too, how lucky we were, not the luck of the angler, but the luck of being born in a place with wild public land to enjoy.

The next day, we drove to the waters draining off into the Great Basin. As we topped a hill, I watched the odometer on my old white truck roll over to 200,000, and I thought about all those miles and all those places I'd been. No place was as special as this one.

Then we were on another water, casting for pure Bonneville cutts. I landed one and took a picture, then caught another. I spent two hours on the stream, drifting between beaver ponds and long beautiful runs with deep holes. We saw another fisherman carrying a good one for supper—a fish probably sixteen inches in length. I made my way to the truck. Janet had still not caught hers and we watched from the road as she cast, and cast again, her jaw set tight, body tense. Finally, a small Bonneville rose to her fly and she had number three.

The years have drifted by like mayfly spinners on a slick run. Much has changed for Wyoming's pure trout. In that meadow near the Thorofare where we camped and saw so few others, an outfitter now runs two-dozen head of livestock and beats the ground down to bare soil. He runs big camps and flies a huge plastic banner between lodgepole pines. The runs of Yellowstone cutts up out of the lake are thinner—and the causes are many: drought, over-fishing, mackinaw in the lake, whirling disease.

In the Wyoming Range, drought plagues the small streams and the large, and the rapid pace of gas development has set its sights on the wildflower-peppered meadows, sage- and aspen-cloaked ridges, and stream banks of the range.

Yet there is still a place called Wyoming. A special place with long summer days, good friends, cold beer, and pure trout. Let us hope that place and those fish will be there for our children. And theirs.

Last Call

Grasshoppers whirl at my feet like playing cards snapped into a stiff wind, a sound that is enough like a rattlesnake to skip my heart a couple of beats. This is snake country, and they are still active, even now with mornings frosted and the aspens stripped naked. I tell the white setter to watch out and stay close to my side.

We have only a few hours of light left in the afternoon and one thousand feet to descend. The air seems frenetic, everything sun-baked, hot, late in the day and year. Even the hoppers seem hurried. Or maybe it's just me.

Most people are hunting elk and deer, but the river calls. I can't hear it from way up here, but it sings to me. I know the flow is low enough now to wade and the water clear enough to fish. The last hoppers are on, defying autumn. Go. Headlamp in the pack, hair-and-feather hoppers tied the past winter in the box, cold dinner of elk salami and Havarti in the bag. Go.

So we drop off the rim, and I can feel the pain of it in my quads almost immediately, half jogging, power hiking down into the canyon. There is a faint game trail that someone, damn them, has flagged with plastic tape. My secret place discovered. I've been scrabbling down into this canyon every year for ten years. This is my one trip for the year, and this one only a few hours squeezed between walls of sheer limestone. Not many make the effort. There are easier fish and gentler places.

I stop long enough to yank the flagging down and call the dog off a family of grouse he's pointing. The trail fades and then disappears, and I'm in the thick north-side Doug fir with gravity as my only guide. I ignore the feel of my toes hammering into the boots. Is that a hot spot developing? To heck with it.

Finally, the river. It is squashed down here, flowing season's-end-low through limestone boulders shed from the top. The river pools, then rushes, twisting. Both banks are too steep and tangled to hike. The river is the only path and only if you are willing to get wet. I rig the fly rod and tie on a hopper, wading into the first pool, heading upstream. The dog stays at my side, pointing fish now instead of birds, happy to be trembling in cold water, watching the trout rise.

The first is a brown, ten inches, sides sprinkled like he's been rolled in black pepper and cayenne. The fight on the two-weight is brief, fun, then over. The next is a rainbow, complete with rainbow acrobatics. The next is a brookie. And so it goes, good fishing in clear water with big flies. Reward for sweat. Made sweeter by the effort of the hike, the urgency of the late hour and season. We wade upstream in the shade of the canyon walls, in the fading light of an October day.

By the time I fish back downstream to my stowed pack, I can no longer see the hopper riding the waves. The hike out, up, will be in moonlight and headlamp. We will take our time on the climb, however, for now there is only sleep ahead.

Fall comes with a quickening in the heart. You smell it early, maybe. Even in the hot years, perhaps as early as August. It happens suddenly. One morning you are standing on your front porch sipping your coffee and it dawns on you how cool it is. There's a smell in the air, too, a smell of grass cured by the sun, of leaves, of sap, of faint thin wood smoke. Now your attention turns to the aspens on the hill above town and to the alder along the creek, watching, waiting for them to signal the beginning of it.

One morning, you notice a thin line of ice on the horse trough, like salt rimming a margarita glass. It won't be long. Not long now. You start to dream when you are awake, just as you did back in April. They were vivid conscious dreams of salmonflies and caddis and trout rising above willow-blanketed islands. Dreams of summer coming. But now your dreams are laced with the smell of wet, happy dog, of elk bugling, of leaves changing and falling, of grouse warm and sun-dappled in your hand, of gunpowder and dog bell.

Autumn is a season that sings of harvest and bounty. Yet, on some days, it is still hot and sweat streams down the center of your back and you worry about hanging meat and fret about blowflies and rattlesnakes and loud leaves crunching under your boots. But it is time to harvest and there is not much time. Most days leave you happy, harvesting, collecting, breathing those great smells.

And yet with fall comes a sadness that washes over you for no apparent reason until you realize you are mourning the good things of summer lost. Still, you remind yourself of the peril of this melancholy path, of the fact that summers, like loves, are remembered only for the good things. Summer may be gone, but gone, too, are the blistering long, hot days, the parched landscapes, the mosquitoes, the horseflies, and the rivers with water too warm and low for healthy trout.

Early on, you look at your calendar and cross out days. You've hoarded your vacation time for this season and the Xs made by your pen take up days, then weekends and finally, whole weeks. Bird hunting. Antelope hunting. Berry picking. Wood gathering. Bird hunting. Harvesting the garden. Canning. Elk hunting. Deer hunting. More bird hunting. Listening to the Denver Broncos and the Wyoming Cowboys on AM radio. Hauling hay. More wood. You are awash in a frantic river of activity and then it hits you.

Fishing. You almost forgot fishing.

Autumn fly fishing is for the dedicated. The rivers have cooled and the action, at least the action of humans, has chilled a bit as well. Most have gone home and are settling into a season of football and cheese dip. So here, at long last, you have the rivers to yourself. If you are lucky, the hoppers will still be going, sometimes as late as mid-October. And if you are really lucky, the big browns will be on the move.

In late October, from the Miracle Mile to the Big Horn to the Green, the fish that we have credited with legendary intelligence, a trout worthy of kings—King Brown himself—will be on the move.

They run into the rivers from the reservoirs and up the rivers into the streams, and up the streams to the cricks. In October, it is entirely possible to catch a brown trout as long as the crick is wide. Big spawners, with sides as yellowed as the meat of a ponderosa pine. If you tie into one of them on your new four-weight, you'll pray for its spine, its soul, and thank gawd that the manufacturer has a breakage guarantee, and you thought to bring a back-up rod.

The big brown boys of autumn react quickly to well-presented flies, as if enjoying the cooling of the water. They'll slash and slam into grasshoppers and other big dries, while beneath the surface, they hammer Montana nymphs, girdle bugs, and woolly buggers. There's nothing subtle about a fall-run brown trout. They have sex on the brain, and like bull elk, thinking about sex can get them into trouble. No longer are they delicately sipping those size 22 midges on 7X tippet. Instead, they'll knock the snot out of a size 6 muddler fished on 4X and leave a hole in the water that seems to take forever to fill back up.

Rainbows and cutthroats, too, seem to frolic in the cooling waters, taking some of the smaller stuff on top, perhaps following the spawn of their brown cousins, perhaps just feeling the urgency of the shortened days. Brook trout run now as well, wearing colors almost too gaudy for nature, reds and blues and greens. They are hungry, and they act quickly and seemingly without premeditation.

The beauty of fall fly fishing is you can wait for the sun to come up over the rimrock before you leave the truck. You can wait for the waters to warm a bit and for the scattered hatches to come on, for the frost to metamorphose into dew, before you rig up and pull on the waders.

You'll fish well, for the whole summer of fishing is behind you and your moves are practiced and honed by solstice-length days.

This short fall day finds you moving carefully among spooky trout, false casting just enough to get the job done, easing over boulders slick with the dying algae of summer. In the cool water, the fish you land fight vigorously and swim off defiantly, still full of spark. Each one you land has you wondering, Is this the last one? Is this the last trout I'm going to land this year?

If you have planned your day well and have had enough smarts to leave the shotgun and bird dogs at home on this rare fall day, you will perhaps—midday and six trout landed—have enough time and the good sense to sit on the bank for a while. Here you can contemplate the vicissitudes of the sporting life in this urgent, too-short, best-of-all-seasons season. You'll watch golden aspen leaves spinning boat-like in the water and once in a while, you'll rise to your feet and cast again. You may even have planned well enough to have packed a lunch into your fly vest. Perhaps, you'll take a break from this quickening of season, from that hurried feel in your heart.

But more likely, you'll fish hard and return many trout to the water and then you'll start to think about that dog. It sure would be nice to put him on some ruffed grouse today.

Soon

Autumn ended in January, and with it came that same old wash of emotion that has followed you like a lonesome dog almost all of your life. It is melancholy. Hunting season has ended.

This one ended on a patch of Nevada lava rock and cheatgrass. It ended with the final bark from the 20-gauge over/under, a hurried, swingless poke at a zipping chukar partridge. A miss. You didn't want to end on a miss. It would have been much sweeter to see the bird jump and watch it in slow-motion. They say Ted Williams could see the stitching on baseballs hurled his way as he swung that big bat, and sometimes, you see birds this way, all details, individual feathers, that bandit chukar partridge mask, the shotgun coming to the shoulder, pulling the trigger in one smooth stroke that you don't even feel. This was not one of those occasions, and you knew you had missed even before the gun came to your shoulder and you know that is why.

But the last chukar jumped and you missed and then the sun was dipping over the far rim and you were thinking of barrel-aged whiskey poured over ice chips and a good cigar smoked by a sage fire. The high-desert winter slipped through your wool shirt and chilled the sweat at the base of your spine and you shouldered your gun, called the dog to heel, and headed down the thin, hard ridge to the valley below and the truck there. And there is that sadness on your shoulder, a familiar old friend. It's over. Last hunt. It's over.

Your sporting life is marked by the tide of seasons. Autumn parallels the hunt, starting in late August when you crawl through the Sweetwater sage pushing your muzzleloader before you, stalking speed goats. Fall days are flanked by Absaroka spruce and bugling bull elk, by the sun dipping down over Wyoming's tallest peak while you bend to the knife work on a cow elk, by pheasants bursting from a mad tangle of wild rose, by a damned good mountain horse beneath you sure and true on a twisting mountain trail. You go trout hunting too and you cast drowned hoppers between boats of cottonwood leaves and occasionally pin the tough toothed jaw of a big brown on the spawn, fighting hard against bent graphite and stretched plastic, splashing to net and let go into near-ice water. The hunt continues, in the good years, through January—Nevada chukar—or even, in really good years, mid-February—Arizona quail.

Some years, life takes over your passion and swallows it, and your autumn ends too soon, in the frozen cattails of a Montana December or on the icy Big Horn where big greenheads paddle among the bergs.

And so. Winter. It stretches out before you and there's a cold wind carrying snow out of the north, and even south. There is no promise of anything much at all except whiteness and chill. There are a woodstove and a huge pile of Doug fir and pine stacked against the side of the house and hay in the barn and meat in the freezer. Nothing to do but wait it out.

So you pull old books off the shelf and page through, smelling the mustiness of time, feeling the leather bindings in your hands, and dancing your eye across the pages. Here you travel up desert ridges, ride wild rivers, feel shale beneath your boots in high mountain holds and you dream. Sometimes, you think of going out into the shrill wind. You could shoot rabbits, but then you reflect on the feather and fin and fur of the past year and you think: That was enough. That was enough. When the books are marked and closed, the scent of gun oil and solvent hits your nostrils, and you feel that sadness again when you wipe a thin coat of oil on the barrel of that good rifle that shot so true not so long ago. You put that rifle back in its place, knowing you will not touch it for some time, and you clean your knives and repair that hole in the pannier that was caused by a young first-time packhorse not familiar with his new width on a narrow trail.

One night, as the wind pushes sheets of snow against the north wall and the old Round Oak wood stove crackles with butter-yellow ponderosa, something happens. You reach the end of a sentence and you stop. You put down that good book, carefully marking the page, and you stand. From the hearth, the cat and the setters eye you: Something is up with the boss.

The lonesome dog is gone. In its place is a happy pup, a healthy chunk of excitement full of eagerness and anticipation. You walk to the back bedroom where the fly vise has been gripped on the tying bench, untouched for a whole summer and autumn. You sit down. You dig out a No. 4 hook, and scratch around for material. And you start to tie. A big fly. Big enough for a big fish.

You have kept materials from the harvest season—materials from animals and birds you shoot. Patches of elk hair for elk hair caddis. Skins of partridge for soft hackles. The neck of a grizzly-hackled rooster that a friend's black Lab chased down and strangled to death in his own barnyard.

Hey, can I have that rooster's skin? Unless you tie, it was an odd request indeed. But if you do, you know.

But the fruits of harvest and mishap are all laid out before you now, salted and seasoned to be spun onto hook and tied with colorful thread. You are not an expert by any means—tying parachutes is begging frustration—but as snow blasts against the west window, you sit warm and sip Kentuck whisky and tie flies for the coming year. There is something poetic and right and good about sitting at a fly vise using feathers from birds that brought you so much enjoyment months earlier, hair from the hide of an elk you shot cleanly and thanked for giving her life so you can enjoy elk steak broiled on a hot outdoor grill. It feels good, to use the animal and the bird like this, to eat a good meal because of it, and to use its clothing to catch fish. There is a self-sufficiency to it like having a compost pile and a good garden coming strong in the spring, like picking chokecherries for jam and syrup in the fall, like burning wood to heat the house. The days and weeks filter by now quickly, gone is that sad dog.

The book goes unopened, the vise unused one night and you look at maps. You dream of pack trips into large country, of mountain lakes with big Yellowstone cutts swimming strong and selectively through clear water. You look at blue lines on maps, country you haven't seen yet and have threatened to hike into for years. You'll go this summer. The next week, you pull out a calendar and stroke the pen across days, weeks. And there's a whole spring ahead too.

Soon, you think, you will be camping beneath fragrant ponderosa and painting chalk across the tongue of the call, then working the lost yelp for that big gobbler you saw two nights before. Soon you will be riding horseback over open sage where the antlers of the previous autumn have fallen, smelling those damned fine fragrances of leather and horse and sweet sage. Soon you will be at the oars, carefully stroking backwater just slow enough so that your friend can cast that big fly you just tied the other night to the place where that big brown has stuck its mouth up like a catcher's mitt. Soon.

Luck

The parking lot promises a crowd. You remember last year, the cars and SUVs at the head of the canyon. You saw the windshields shining before you turned down the dirt road and you gulped. Cars from everywhere, cars from the cities and from corn country. But down in the canyon, no one. This year will be the same, although the clot of cars makes you shake your head and wish for another time when you fished the stream and there was no one, not even in the parking lot.

You walk then, pulling your Sage four-weight together and stringing line as you walk. Without being at the creek, or seeing what is going on down on the water, you twist a knot through a bead-head pheasant's tail nymph.

You see the first fisherman where the trail hits the stream. You make no move to find a place to fish. You walk. Through sage and blue flag, past penstemon thick with bud and promise. Grasshoppers launch into the sage, a few ones, small, nothing big enough or abundant enough for you to stop and tie on a hopper pattern instead of the bead-head. You see another group of fishermen spread out just wide enough so they can shout fishing success back and forth and still you walk, nodding at them, passing a word or two of fishing report back and forth and you move on. They are dressed in waders and fly vests, not prepared for a longer walk into the canyon. That's two groups. Five cars. There should be more ahead and you go on, drinking from the water bottle in your pack, walking fast.

The sage scrapes against your bare legs and a rock works its way into your tennis shoes, but you press on. You will wade wet, braving the melt of early summer snow. Waders would be nice but you need the mobility of shorts and tennis shoes and will sacrifice cold legs and numb toes for a fast walk down a twisted canyon.

You pass a lone fisherman and you stand and watch for a while. It is a young guy wearing a straw hat, and he casts beautifully and mends his line on the water. You tear yourself away from the scene and move on, over clumps of cactus and sage, through alder and willow thickets, past lichened granite.

The canyon drops and you see another fisherman, then another. That, you think, could be the last of them and you walk farther. Your fly line is still dry. The big fish and the better fishing are farther down.

Finally the stream. It runs to your thighs and is the color of black tea baked in a hot sun. It is not the color you were hoping for, a little dingier, more sullen, than a good fly-fishing stream should be. But you have walked all this way and you work the fly out of the keeper and lay out a long stream of line in a perfect, coordinated cast, thinking, Not bad for the first cast of the summer. The fly bumps along, ticking the bottom, rolling with the current. You cast again. And again. Again.

No fish takes the bead head, but you don't quit. You are alone and you know that these fish have not seen too many fishermen. You are too far down the canyon, have worked too hard for this and you will not retreat in your quest. Finally, though, you reel in and take up the wet line in your left hand, feeling the water stream off your fingers, checking the leader for wind knots—you've tied two—and looking over the nymph. A fluttering by your ear makes you change your mind about the fly on the end of your line. It is a big bug, a salmon fly, and somehow, it flies. It looks too big to fly, prehistoric somehow, awkward. Dinosaurs shouldn't fly but pterodactyls did and this one does too. It is not surprise that the names of both creatures start with pt: pterodactyl and pteronarcys. It's as long as your little finger and you watch it helicopter up over the willows and disappear. For a while, you watch the hole in the sky where it was and you wonder if perhaps you imagined that huge insect, if you dreamed it up in your fish-crazed mind. Then another one comes in low, barely skimming over the water, and you stand open-mouthed, watching it. You think you'll hear a huge splash, a gulp and a hole will be left in the water where a brown as long as your forearm rose and sucked the bug into its maw. But nothing happens and this salmon fly, too, flies off to breed.

Hurriedly, you spin the knot around a big fat orange Stimulator. It's the biggest thing in your box, not as long as your pinkie finger, but long enough. You hope. You dress it with floatant and make a few hesitant casts and lay it on the stream. It bobs well, and you can even see it when you cast it into the sun and the light slivers off into the sky and your eye. Still, you can see it and you lean forward into the drift, pointing the rod tip and the fly, waiting, waiting.

You cast again. Nothing. There is nothing going on. The bugs are out now, not thick. Not a hatch, per se, but still the bugs are out and surely something should be hammering the fly. It's really not that far off from the real thing.

You fish for an hour, then eat lunch. It's a sandwich of roasted garlic, left-over elk steak from last night's grill and thick sharp Vermont cheese. It is your attempt to eat right and you lie back and listen to a vireo trilling from an alder and chew on the soggy bagel sandwich. You watch the big stones floating in the wind up and down the stream and still, nothing is doing. Nothing on the surface, nothing below. You roll up onto an elbow and you debate the next move and finally rise and cast. It's a beautiful cast and the fly rides high on riffle and wave and still nothing. You decide to change and casually, lazily, the fly trails off into the current and hangs there at the end of your line, bouncing in its own wake, the current pulling on your rod. You thumb through your fly box, and find a San Juan worm. Mighty close to bait, but what the hell, and as you lift your rod to grab the leader so you can clip off the Stimulator, you notice a weight at the end of the line and you set the hook. It's a brown and it takes to the air, and dances on its tail and then runs into deep water and you hold the rod high and stuff the fly box into your shirt pocket with the other hand and you fight him for a while, perhaps a minute, maybe five. And the shallow back eddy is there and you gently remove the hook and he flicks back out into deep current. A big, nice, fat brown.

"It's a bit like life, isn't it?" you say aloud. Work hard getting there, go one step farther than most, pause occasionally to admire the work of a peer, and then work at your task all day long to no avail. In the end, sometimes, it all comes down to just a little bit of luck.

Fishing Dogs

I've always been something of an outdoors schizophrenic. This does not mean a crazy person who lives outside. Nor does this imply that I only go nuts when I'm out of the house. No, what I am is a person who has too many interests to fit into a lifetime and most of those interests are spent in wild country. Finding time to enjoy as many of those interests as possible—and still hold down a job that pays for it all—leaves one a tad bit tired, if not a little insane. Fly fishing, boating, canoeing, bird and big game hunting, telemark skiing, horsepacking, backpacking. Only one lifetime.

Some of these activities fit together seamlessly. Canoeing and fishing are two perfect examples. Other activities just don't belong in the same drift boat—kind of like trying to make a marriage between a cat fancier and a breeder of killer pit bulls work. There are many times when I feel that taking dogs along on a fishing trip is that kind of ill-fitting hat.

True, if you hunt birds and fly fish, there are some real advantages. Pheasant and Hungarian partridge skins really come in handy for fly tying. But actually taking that same dog who pointed those rooster pheasants last fall out fly fishing this summer can be a bit more problematic.

After a lot of years spent trying to marry these two unlikely partners, I've boiled my "taking dogs fishing" philosophy down to a couple of quick caveats: Take the right dog. Go by yourself unless your dog is really well trained. Take a dog that really doesn't like water. And leave him at home if you are really serious about catching fish.

Taking the right dog is absolutely critical. Several years ago, I decided to step out and buy a drift boat. I'd been wanting one for years and one doesn't get by in a state like Montana without some kind of watercraft. When a good one came up for sale in the local paper two weeks after I'd moved to Montana, a friend and I jumped on it. The first trip, we floated an easy stretch of river with another friend who knew his way around oar-powered craft. Neither of the new owners knew a thing. But, with a little coaching, we felt like pros after only one day.

That next day came with just the two of us and no coach. We decided to tackle the upper Madison which is one long, boulder-strewn riffle. For a skilled boater, the river is one of the finest in the country. For the tender, it is a nightmare. I brought my two English setters: Ike, a big male, and Sage, an energetic female.

We launched. Thankfully, it was early spring and not many people were out to see the ridiculous events of that day. My friend took the oars first and we pivoted out into the stream, spun in a 360 and slammed into a big boulder. The water was not that fast. Ike immediately went to the bottom of the boat in a quivering, wet bundle of nerves. Sage hopped to the bow and watched geese fly over. We slammed into another rock. Ike tried to crawl under the oarsman's seat. I tightened my life jacket. We slammed into another rock, spun in another 360 and my usually-unsullied friend unleashed a string of obscenities that would make Andrew Dice Clay blush. Sage wagged her tail from the bow and watched the water for rising trout. Ike trembled wet in the bottom of the boat.

We made it down the river that day, which is obvious because I'm alive to write the tale, but it was one long day with moments sheer terror on the part of one dog and two inept captains interspersed with absolute effervescence on the part of little Sage. On that day, Sage became my boat dog. I've gotten a whole lot better at the sticks and these days, when I take out the drift boat, Ike stays home and Sage is the queen of her own ship.

Which brings me to my second point: Make sure your dog is really well trained if you insist on taking him or her fishing. Not long after that epic harrowing journey through Class Six whitewater on the Madison, Sage joined another friend and I on a much milder river and I actually hooked a fish from the boat. While I was playing the fish and getting ready to net it—it was only about a fourteen-inch rainbow—I wasn't paying attention to Sage. She was intent upon the action and as the fish splashed near my net, all of a sudden, she was overboard in an effort to retrieve it. Now I was playing a fish with one hand and trying to grab the dog out of the water with the other. Then I was trying to keep the fish away from the dog. Then I lost the fish. Had it been a four-pounder, I might have been a little hot. But as it was, I learned a valuable lesson. Now when I'm playing a fish near the boat, I always make sure I know where Sage is and give her words of advice. She usually listens.

A well-trained dog is critical. Don't get me started on other people's dogs. If it's your boat, you can bring a dog. If you are driving, you can bring a dog. But if you are going with someone else who is doing the steering and using their boat, you had better just leave the critter at home. At the minimum, you had better ask your friend, and you absolutely need a dog that listens. Otherwise, go alone with your dog.

Ike is a pretty darned good wading dog. He'll work at heel all day long while I fish and he'll rarely get far out into the water. I took him by himself on a week-long horseback trip into a Montana wilderness one summer. We fished lakes and small streams and Ike stayed at my side the whole time. He, too, has the occasional tendency to ignore his natural "setter-born-I-hate-water" tendencies and leap out into it when I am playing a fish. But with one or two words, he'll stay on the bank.

This is mostly because setters really don't like water. That's a big advantage for a good fishing dog. I avoid fishing with Labs. While I once had a springer-lab named JD who was a pretty good fishing dog, water dogs and fishing are not a very good fit. Nothing puts down rising fish like fifty pounds of black fur hitting the water at fifty miles per hour. Setters and other water-wimps actually can intently watch the action and even become fish pointers. I have a friend who was fishing a rise and was so intent on the trout that he lost track of his setter. Then he got a strange sensation that something was watching him from the bank and he looked up to see his big male setter locked up tight in the bank-side willows, intent upon the feeding fish—a trout pointer.

I recently added a third dog to the crew and last summer I took young Echo out on the boat for the day. He had a good time and he has the makings of a boat dog. Now I have a pack of three setters and they are fine companions. But if you are really wanting to spend time on the water fishing, looking at the hatches, watching the rises, working the fish just right, then leave the pooch at home. If you want to concentrate on fishing fully and getting lost in it, then the canine companion is best saved for the fields of autumn and not the riffles of June.

High Water

The mountain river shoulders up out of its banks, pushing into the willows and alder, washing flotsam upon new grass. The water, though, is clear. But it is big and fast and the run-out is not good: miss your footing on slippery stone and it is down through Class V with only the air in your lungs for flotation and flailing arms for locomotion. This is early summer fishing in high Montana, and tall water is part of it.

This day threatens rain, and it is the kind of day that never produces. It never warms enough for a hatch, it never squeezes enough moisture out of the clouds to matter much at all, and it never produces a fish. It does produce cold wind from the granite and snow flanks of the mountain to the west and it also does produce a particularly dandy batch of hungry mosquitoes that somehow thrive despite the cold that deters other bugs. Not even the wind can keep them down. They hang in the leeward side of your body and dine. Later, down out of the high country, you will wonder why all the bites are on one side and then you'll remember the mosquitoes surfing in the wake of your body.

It is not always this tough on this river. There have been days of good casting and a steady rise of big fish. This time of the year the big rainbows usually show up, running up out of the desert river below, and eating little fish, slapping and slurping on the water. On a few of these days you've caught them, chunky specimens of pink and green. Just last year, you had your best year and you netted six rainbows, all over 18 inches, all thick sinew and strong gill. Brawlers in a mountain river of high water.

Since there is little else to do other than practice casting into the wind, you find a convenient stump, a gray strong thing that has been polished by the mountain winds and etched by winter storms. It is a good place for a cigar, and the smoke clouds into the wake of your frame and drives the mosquitoes to less heavily armed prey. And you think about high water.

And abundance.

Now is the time. *Carpe diem.* If you do not live in the now, right now, then you will be missing the whole point. There has never been a better time in modern history to take a fly rod in hand and cast to the trout feeding thick in clear pools. There has never been a better time to heft a good rifle or shotgun and go afield for game, furred and feathered all.

Now is the time. Those of us who fight and whine and complain about things beyond our immediate control are cautioned to remember that whining and complaining takes time and energy. Time and energy that are better spent enjoying what makes you live where it's tough to survive, brought you here and keeps you here. Certainly, don't forget to fight, but don't forget why you fight. This is the reason you are here, to cast on good water and cast your eyes across a mountain hold. And these are the high water years. Make no mistake. In fact, some of the high water may already be receding, never to be seen again. It is likely that we will never see the big mule deer boom of the 1960s ever again.

Perhaps we will never see chukar and gray partridge in the numbers of the 1990s. Clearly, the sage grouse will not be back to the 1920s levels.

But for all we have lost and for all that is past, it is still good to be a modern-day Montana sportsman. There are elk in abundance. In many places you can tag two in a year. You can even shoot a wild bison if you are lucky enough to draw a permit. There are good fish in streams and lakes that never held trout before white man came to this land. You can still catch pure subspecies of native trout. You can even catch fish that are native to places like California's Sierra Nevada (golden trout), Germany (brown trout), or the Midwest (walleye). There are solid numbers of mule deer, whitetail deer and antelope, and there are moose in places there never were moose before.

We sportsmen have more and enjoy more than any man in the history of mankind. Right now is high water. Enjoy it now, because we are placing a lot of demand on the land that has given us so much already; this generation is living and consuming as if there will not be a next.

Right now. Get out there. The water is dropping.

Off

The carnival was in town when she moved out. Across the park. I could see it there at the fairgrounds, a moving, noisy mass of machinery screaming. People screaming. Eating things like turkey legs and colored sugar spun into cotton candy and then hopping on a ride that had just been assembled off the semi truck by some cat with tattoos up his neck, summer teeth*, piercings and a nice little meth habit.

She left me a note, not an explanation: "Thanks! We had some fun. I left you the boat. Enjoy!"

I went off to work that morning and came home and she was gone.

The only thing the note lacked was smiley faces and hearts. Lots of exclamation. No explanation. Maybe, I told my buddy, she ran off with the carnival. I was only half kidding.

"Dude. She left you a boat."

Perspective.

It is an inflatable one-man pontoon. New. Never even been on the water. Never been assembled. Never been inflated. There had been some thought of getting one myself, for the small rivers, too small for the drift boat. The Stillwater. The Boulder. The Greybull. Even the Beaverhead in some places. Real boaters hate them. But they do look like fun. Kind of like riding a moped. Fun to ride. Don't want your buddies catching you in the act.

We had been talking about going into the Crazies when I left just that morning. Climbing up a trail, fishing up a stream, heading to a high lake with Yellowstone cutts or goldens. But when I came home only a few hours later, she, and all of her stuff—enough to pack her red Honda Civic to the gills four months ago when she moved in—was gone. All of it. All trace. The only evidence that she'd ever lived with me was the uninflated pontoon boat in the garage. The Crazies. Huh.

More perspective. "Hey, how about we come over this weekend and go fishing with you? Take your mind off things?"

There's a blue line not far from my house. You can ride your bike to it, and thanks to Montana's access law, hop in the stream and start fishing. Right past someone's front porch. I like that concept, fishing right past someone's front porch. Catching fish while the man of the house is grilling a T-bone.

VD and his girlfriend, Abby, showed up just as the pale morning dun hatch was coming off. We scrambled down beneath the bridge and started wading upstream. I cast a beautiful nine-foot three-weight, a precision instrument for small streams and tight spots. The length, rather than a disadvantage in tight spots and small streams, was actually an advantage. You can reach over and under things, and drop flies into holes the size of a coffee can. Problem was, I wasn't.

I was off. Badly. I cast okay, and the fly hit the water, but I just was not catching anything. I was anything but Zen. I was not into it, caught up in thought, drifting aimlessly, not concentrating. We leap-frogged each other up the small stream, the three of us, spreading out. The stream runs past a golf course, and I cast into a pool with two stray Titleists stuck like little white emerging mushrooms half-buried in mud. A bad slice or two, obviously. We could hear the Pink! sound of metal hitting ball and laughter as we worked our way upstream, sheltered by a wall of willow from seeing the course and its players.

VD hooked a fish. A trophy whitefish. It fought hard and deep and then came to the net, all of twenty inches. Abby took a nice brown at the head of the next pool and then it was my turn. I threw the same thing as they, but nothing tapped my line. I switched to a nymph, fished eighteen inches below a strike indicator, and cast twenty, thirty times into a beautiful bent run. Not a tick. VD stepped into the same run, fishing two Prince Nymphs. Harry and William. He hooked a good fat rainbow, fought it, and unpinned it without taking it out of the water. Abby was up and struck, missed. Then hit. Another nice brown. My turn. Nothing.

I'm definitely off. Distracted. Trying not to think about things, trying to think about fishing, about being present rather than past—although this past is less than forty-eight hours old. I'm incredulous most of the time, wondering what in the heck happened. Thinking about going off to work and her in the house, scrambling to pack stuff into her car before I could return. Running from something. Wondering if she even said goodbye to my bird dogs. I try to work through it, casting. It ain't working.

The PMDs ride in clouds above the stream but there's little action on top. The fish seem to be on nymphs instead.

For a long time, we walk up the stream, casting, taking turns. I don't turn a fish, lost in thought again and drifting more. Off.

We work upstream past the golf course to a place where the stream bends sharply into a thick bank of black soil, the water pushing up against the bank, the sod falling in coffee-table–sized chunks down into the water. The stream pools around the sod, making little pockets. Perhaps a little cover for trout. Behind one of these thick sod chunks, we see a rise, a trout working an area no bigger than the seat of a chair. I am up.

I've switched to a PMD, a size 18. I haven't turned, rolled or stung a fish all day. VD and Abby watch from downstream. I strip out line, looking at the spot, strip out more line, measuring, gauging the distance, and drop the fly perfectly in the spot. It floats twelve inches, I mend perfectly, dragless, and the fish comes up and the strike is lifted into its mouth. It is on. It fights hard, jumping, spinning. The cast, the hook-set, and the fish is at hand. Then released. All of it in perfect symmetry, perfect timing. I look up at VD and Abby and grin. VD, as if reading my thoughts, grins. "That's more like it, man. Hey. She left you a boat."

Guess I better get the thing pumped up.

* Summer teeth: n. Some are in his head and some ain't.

In Praise of Mighty Whitey

I'm not sure when I started wanting to own a drift boat. I do know why. On various trips around Wyoming or to Montana or Idaho, I'd drive past glimmering rivers and catch an occasional glimpse of a drift boat, anglers fore and aft, a hardy captain at the oars. It was a dream that I carried for a number of years until finally, one bright spring day, I saw an advertisement in the local paper: 2001 Clacka, fully equipped. The price was right and I had a buddy who had also dreamed drift boat dreams, so we pooled our money and ended up with a fine craft. Now we were in perfect position to catch trout after trout, to bring brawling rainbows and brawny browns to net as we floated in a Captain Morgan pose down some frothy western river.

The first fish on the first voyage was a whitefish.

So was the second fish. And the third. In fact, other than one brown coming off a poor winter, all the fish we caught were whitefish. While many anglers might have thought this a poor day on the water, we reckoned that we'd had a pretty fine first day and in fact from that point on, our fine craft became the SS *Whitefish*.

Whitefish for me have been as much a part of fishing as trout. Being a western kid, raised on public land, tanned beneath a wide sky, I've always caught whitefish when I've been seeking trout. I've caught trout when I've been in pursuit of whitefish. They are fine dining, smoked with hickory or mesquite. They are good fighters and they take a nymph drifted naturally in pure current. And, for me, they are a symbol of the Wild West, a pure native fish that has more business in a Western river than do the foreigners like German browns, Eastern brookies, and Pacific Northwestern rainbows. Whitefish and cutthroat trout evolved side-by-side in western waters.

I caught my first whitefish in my native Colorado when I was just learning to fly fish. I read *Field and Stream* by flashlight and I taught myself to fly cast from those articles and by waving around a cheap fiberglass Eagle Claw fly rod in my front lawn. The first fish I brought to net were brook trout and the next were whitefish. The latter came on the Elk River out of Steamboat Springs, Colorado, in the summer of '72. I was ten years old. I can still remember that fish, the clear water, the smell of streamside spruce. I ate him.

Through the years, Mr. White has saved many a fishless day. Sure, he's drab. He's kind of slimy. He's got a face only a mother could love. Yet he's likely the proverbial "canary in the coal mine" for water quality. He's a genuine true-blue native Westerner. He's good eating. He's a fighter. What's not to love?

I've never understood why the mountain whitefish, a coldwater game fish native to our western waters, was the object of disdain among some fishermen. Possibly the reason comes from a widespread "take as many as you can" regulation of many game and fish agencies that still allow fifty-fish limits. Wildlife and fisheries management history has shown that high bag limits lead the public to a general feeling of unlimited riches.

Then there's the open disgust that some so-called "sportsmen" on Western rivers have shown whitefish through the years. Stories of fishermen throwing whitefish on the banks, or running objects through their gills, or giving them a firm squeeze before tossing them overboard are abundant. Such actions speak not only of a poor sporting ethic that amounts to poaching, but also of plain ignorance for a native species in native water and a disregard for its place in a coldwater ecosystem.

The irony of a person gently catching and releasing an exotic non-native fish such as a brown or rainbow trout yet killing and wantonly wasting a native is palpable. This is a fish that is classified as a game fish. It is not a trash fish and yet some unethical fishermen treat it as such.

Yet other people will tell you that many a trout-free day on a Western river has been saved by whitefish. Sometimes, when the trout bite is off, Mr. White is the only customer you can catch. They often fight hard and provide the same kind of sport as an equally sized trout. They can be released gently to fight another day and they take bait, small nymphs, the occasional dry and even once in a while a big hopper. The latter happened one summer on the Yellowstone River when my brother came up to visit for three days of fishing. We boated many Yellowstone native cutthroats and many whitefish. It was an all-native day.

A few years ago, a friend and I drew a permit on Montana's Smith River. The legendary Smith, and its even more legendary permit to float, is a trip of a lifetime. But the only problem was, we drew our permit in June right in the height of the run-off. The Smith was about the color of creamed coffee. We launched our canoe anyway, and made our way down between the ponderosa- and trophy-home—lined banks. We fished occasionally, driven by hopeful optimism, but caught nothing in the main Smith. One day, we rounded a bend where one of the river's main tributaries dumps in. It was clear. We wandered up the clear crick, fishing hard, and caught three trout and about a dozen whitefish. The trip was saved.

These have been years of low flows and troubled water systems. The mountain whitefish, that native fish, is looking to be in serious trouble. If you have fished Western rivers for more than a decade, ask yourself if you catch as many whitefish as you used to. Chances are the answer is no and not by a long shot.

The anecdotal evidence of this is everywhere. On Colorado's Frying Pan River, a mountain whitefish tournament used to require at least fifty whiteys to win. In recent years, the winning team caught only eight or nine fish. On the famed Madison, guides had a hard time keeping whitefish off the hook in the '70s and '80s; now whitefish are only occasionally boated.

Mr. White appears to be in serious trouble. Part of the reason may be drought, which is hitting not only whitefish, but also other cold-water species like our beloved trout and imperiled grayling. Another part of the equation is whirling disease. Whirling disease is carried by tubifex worms, and the parasites infect the nervous systems of young fish. The morality rate is high, about 90 percent. Now, initial findings are indicating that whitefish are very susceptible to whirling disease.

Science has a problem and it probably traces back to the widespread disrespect that the whitefish gets from the trout-hunting populace. Not very much is known about whitefish to begin with. Few people have ever studied them. We do know that they are fall spawners and are not sexually mature until they are three years old. We also know that they do not compete much with our trout because they feed near the bottom while trout feed mostly on drifting insects. Where bull trout are part of the river ecosystem, juvenile whitefish are an important food source, with big bull trout snacking on young whitefish like candy. For a rare native fish like bull trout, a good consistent food source like whitefish is key to the survival of an entire species.

Regardless if whitefish save your trout-free day, or if they feed an important species like bull trout, there is not doubt that whitefish are part of the system that makes things work. So while you are out on those beautiful shimmering western rivers and have been stumped by trout, don't "dis" Mr. White. Bring him to the boat, net him gently and release him to fight another day. I, for one, do not want to think of a world without a western native like "Whitey."

Born on the 'Horn

Sometimes in my more pensive and reflective moments, when I'm contemplating the path I have taken and am taking, I imagine my fisherman self was born on the 'Horn. These moments especially come when I am envisioning myself a fish. All anglers, even the most rank (double meaning in that word) of beginners—see themselves in the water, swimming, eating bugs, running with the current. It helps to think of yourself as trout in trout country.

The 'Horn hatches in Wyoming. If I am a trout on the upper reaches of the 'Horn, I am a golden or a cutthroat. I swim in pools formed by the granite knuckles of the Wind River Range. Up here, up high, the Bighorn is known as the Popo Agie, the Little Wind, the Wiggins Fork, Torrey Creek, Dinwoody, Bull Lake Creek. Others. Some too small to have names. Born in glacier ice and annual snowmelt. Pulled by gravity, carving rock, harboring trout and the char called trout, the brookie. Lower down, these streams are rainbow and brown water, good fishing. Sometimes great fishing.

Eventually these streams become the Wind River, a river of high potential for trout fishing, but like many trout rivers of the west, most of it waters alfalfa and sugar beets in wide fields of poor soil. But the river flows into a reservoir and at the tailwater, the river is born again, the Wind in Wind River Canyon. A different personality, one that is clear and shallow in winter and early spring, then runs green and deep and strong and rapid in late spring and summer as irrigation water is released from the dam. It is a brown and rainbow river. You might not catch many fish, but those you will be lucky enough to heft into your net, photograph, and release, will have shoulders. Once in a while, perhaps while stripping a Yuk Bug in the shallow water at the tail of a run, you will feel the hammering strike of something bigger, meaner, unseen. You'll lift your rod tip, feel a frightening tug, once, twice and you'll bend the rod into the fish and line will peel out from beneath your clamped index finger—burning it a bit—and you'll try to regain your composure and then whatever hit your fly will be gone and your fly with it and on 2X no less. All of this much faster than you just read those words. You'll check your shorts, sit on a streamside boulder, shake your head until the trembling ceases and then stand up and tie on another fly. That's the Wind (aka the Bighorn).

At the mouth of this canyon at a place called Wedding of the Waters, the Wind becomes the Bighorn. Why? Because mountain men coming up the river from the north called it the Bighorn and mountain men hitting the river from the east called it the Wind. When the cartographers got together to map out the West, they apparently thought that the pioneers who followed the mountain men would be too thick to understand that the river was one and the same, so they just changed its name at a convenient location and called it good. There's no waters to wed here, there's not even a tributary coming in to "marry" the river. It's just a river being named something else. For several miles from where it is "born" as it flows through the farmland around Thermopolis, the fishing can be tremendous, particularly for browns. But downstream a ways, the river warms and becomes sauger, ling and carp water.

But at the Montana line—rejoice!—another dam. The best dam of all, the dam that births the Bighorn of Bighorns, the famed and infamous 'Horn. It is here where I am in the midst of a feeble attempt to mature as a fly fisherman. If I was born in the high country alongside the headwaters of the baby 'Horn, if I perfected my fish catching here, then on the grown-up 'Horn in Montana, I am learning the fine art of maturing on a fickle river and the higher art of saying, "Well, it's just great to be out on a day like this." And believing it. Or at least convincing myself that I believe that statement.

This is the 43-mile stretch of the Bighorn River that comes out of the bottom of Yellowtail Dam and becomes one of the best trout rivers in the country. While most of the best of the fishing is in the first twelve to sixteen miles, there are trout all the way down to the town of Hardin—though mostly warm-tolerant browns. But in those first sixteen or so miles, you will find clear pools and runs thick with browns and rainbows, some ripped and muscled. The reason the 'Horn is such a good river is because of the water temperature— even in August the 'Horn runs cold enough that you'll need waders. Coupled with abundant biomass—that's a snooty way of saying "food"—it's a fishing Mecca.

The first time I found myself on the 'Horn was a decade ago in late summer. I remember catching fish on hoppers and caddis and having a good day as fishing a new river goes. I didn't catch many though, and while camping up there, we heard rumors that the Beaverhead was fishing well and so we pulled camp and driftboat all the way across a lot of Montana and found fishing that was about as good as it had been on the 'Horn, but not quite. It reminded me of my ski bum days when I chased snow across the West only to discover that the best powder was right back where I had started.

That year, I do remember a particular brown that I caught in a back channel below the Drive-In (named for the Detroit riprap of '50s era Chevys and Fords). I was casting a Stimulator, one of my favorite flies, and working up this small channel while my comrades were fishing the mainstem 'Horn. I landed the "Stimmy" right against the bank, and it floated beneath a willow, the leader threatening to snag in a trailing willow branch—but not—one of those perfect drifts that imprint on your memory. The mouth of a big brown came out of the water, in slow motion. I imagine that the big brown had not moved much all summer; sticking that big upper lip up out of the water and swallowing whatever came his way—drakes and stones and caddis and hoppers and maybe even drowning mice. I calmed myself and set the hook when my fly disappeared and he was on.

He ran into the current strong and upstream and I let him. Not that I had much choice in the matter. I tried to slow him and when he turned and ran past me, I worked him into slower water and I ran after him, splashing, clumsy in waders. By the time he wore down and I slipped him into the net, my mouth was dry and heart hammering away and I laid him up against my rod and took a guess at where his nose quit. I measured that section of rod back at camp and it came to twenty-one inches. Then we left the river looking for something better. There is no figuring the mind of an angler on the hunt. Big browns can do that to you.

I've had other days on the 'Horn with more fish, but smaller. I've had completely fishless days. I've had days when I caught one or two. The river is a conundrum. I think that is what I like about it.

One summer, three of us descended upon the 'Horn, full of that optimism that swells an angler's soul before the boat is launched. I rigged two rods, a seven weight with a big ugly streamer called a Matuka, and a five weight with a San Juan worm and a bead head dropper. I had been on the Madison just a week or two before and the rubber legs/San Juan combo had been deadly. Now it was late enough in the season and my ego was bruised enough from the big rivers that I was embracing the "Worm" as a fly gift, from the heavens. Early season, when fishing fever runs high, the Worm remains in the box—much like the bait that it resembles—held in temporary disdain by a fly guy's arrogance. But days without fish will quickly make you rediscover Don Juan the Worm.

On this day, he failed me. So did the big Matuka. So did everything else that I threw and that my partners threw. What's more, we watched angler after angler in the flotilla of boats that sailed past get bent into fish after fish. It was downright depressing. Finally, my buddy Jason swallowed enough of his pride that he went over and asked. And got a favorable answer. We switched to tiny stuff, size 20s and below. Zebra midges and WD-40s and the like. Two-fly rigs and we started to get into them. We caught a lot of fish that day. Would have caught more if we had swallowed our pride earlier. But there is no figuring the mind of the angler on the hunt or on the 'Horn.

I have a favorite time of year on the 'Horn. I also have a time of year when I'd like to hit it but never have. The latter is late fall, when the browns are on "horned-up" and acting like bull elk in September. I have a friend who is 80-something who makes an annual foray from Wyoming up to Montana for this time of year. He takes a lot of fish. The problem for me is three bird dogs and a lust for things that fly and cackle. Hunting always gets in the way of my fishing deep in the year. Maybe this year, though…I always say that.

But in early spring, before the license plates all turn green, you can really enjoy the 'Horn. The crowds of summer are far off and the river runs clear and cold like it always does. If you get a fish on, you park the boat and fish some more because at this time, they seem to school. Small stuff mostly, drifted slow and deep and a rod tip lifted at even the slightest bump. I like this time of year because the geese are pairing up, the ducks are coming back, and you'll see a bald eagle cruising the sky. Later in the season, you'll hear a lusty rooster calling from the cottonwoods and you'll catch rainbows on the verge of the spawn. And, on a good day, you'll see few other fishermen and the best holes will be clear and there will be no guides to curse at other boaters who dare to be on "their" river. Few people, the wildlife coming alive after a long winter, the fish starting to move and think about reproduction—good times. And, when it is slow and the fish are not cooperating, perhaps there will be a break in the wind and the clouds will part and if you've worn something dark, even black, the sun will warm you. There's nothing like the feel of a thoughtful March sun on a black fleece. At such times, you'll pull out a cigar and sit streamside and contemplate your path and meditate. On the 'Horn.

Chance

There's an old saw that time flies faster the older you get. There was a day when such an admonition would be so much fodder for the belief that pensioners are old fashioned and out of step with reality. How can time somehow get shorter even though the days and nights, weeks and months are the exact length when you are fifty-six or six? An illusion? A trick of light? Some aging pattern in which neuron and synapse begin to deteriorate and the first function in the process is the human understanding of term?

Yet there is truth in the height of the grass growing up through the boat trailer frame. The thick, thorough web of a cat-eye spider spun over the oars and oar locks. The dust on rod tubes stacked in the corner of the office. Somehow, the season evaporated like morning mist on a river.

Summer has gone and with it plans made but never realized, the fishing trips never taken. The wane of the year is upon us with its shortening, leaning light, its tanning grasses and fading leaf. And although there are days that will call us to river and field yet ahead, there is the regret of what was missed and not done, more powerful than the feeling of completed task and accomplished chore.

I did not go fishing one particular day this past summer and it is something I will remember not doing for the rest of my days.

The text came late on a Saturday night. "Big Hole tomorrow???????????? Coming by your place at 7 if you want to go."

I replied with some excuse about a Sunday and a stack of chores and did not think much about my two friends out on the home river as I put a shoulder to a day of work around the place. I have no idea what I did that day, but on that day, it seemed more important than fishing with two good friends.

We were just wrapping up, easing into the long recline before bedtime when the wreck happened. Pastoral relaxation met incomprehensible chaos. A sound of steel on asphalt, tire and glass. Random, strange things flying through the air as if in some movie about the end of the earth. A trick of brain cell and its ability to compute sight and sound into realization of what was actually being seen. Time, conversely, went slowly. Or perhaps this was different visualization of time entirely, as if we were above it somehow, outside, looking in but not in it. A truck, flipping sideways, again and again, out on the highway at the end of the driveway out in front of our little ranch.

"Call 911!!!" A sprint to the end of the driveway out to the highway, a road seldom traveled on a Sunday evening. The first thing: detritus. Stuff. Everywhere. A Yeti cooler had taken out our mailbox. A wader bag hung from a fence post. A fly rod tube, bent at right angles, lay in the horse pasture. A tire and its wheel, disconnected from its axle. Fly boxes and boat bags. Everywhere the rubble of explosion. And still the brain lacking understanding, the moment somehow, some way, frozen. A twisted hunk of metal of what might have been a flatbed pickup truck, but might not have been. Maybe some craft dropped out of that apocalyptic movie. The cab almost completely off the chassis. Driver's window rolled up. Windshield shattered, but intact. Passenger window down. No one inside the cab. Look down the road. There. At least seventy feet away from the truck. There in the borrow pit. Lying face up, twisted like metal, broken like that rod tube. Run. Seconds in the camouflage of hours. A body. Run to it. Not breathing. Look again. And then the brain works, computes, realizes. It's Dave. Dave on his way home alone after a day of fishing. It's Dave and he's dead.

Somewhere, lost in two decades, is training. Clear an airway. Stabilize the head. It's all you can do. On the knees in a borrow pit on the side of a Montana country road, comes the realization that this is the fishing trip I turned down and here in my hands, is my fishing buddy's life and there is no breath in that life and all I can do is clear and stabilize and wait for the professionals.

Then he takes a breath. And another. And another. The world becomes a space where the only important thing is his breathing. And, not moving. One. Single. Muscle. Fifty minutes go by and the world around us is chaotic and disconnected, feet and legs and flashing colorful lights and just so much noise. A chopper and then help. Finally. Finally help. Fifty minutes disguised as fifty days.

Weeks later, after a long, hard journey for our friend and his family, I see a missed call on my cell phone. It had been one of those days when things were popping left and right, the phone ringing and sending all messages to voice mail and more happening by the minute.

Hours later, I listened to the message and time slowed once more. "This is Dave. I just wanted you to know that I spent the day hugging and kissing on my little girls and I want to thank you for saving my life so I can spend the rest of my life doing that."

So a fishing trip was not taken this summer. I wonder what would have happened if I had gone that day. How the timing of steps can take one from a fateful moment to the humdrum. How there are connections in this universe that we will never understand. How time is marked by life-changing events, friendships, fishing trips taken and not. On some days, time is measured by a pulse and graphed by a machine in a hospital. Some days are forgettable and some seconds last forever. How life is comprised of only so many heartbeats and every one is precious. And I circle back to that old saying about time going faster.

And the other half that goes along with it: so enjoy every moment of it.

Ginna

If you walked south from the house toward the mountain you would find the path there winding between gooseberry and currant and mountain mahogany. In late summer, the path would be worn dusty by the tread of the boy and the grandmother and if you were a tracker, you might see things. Like the pattern of the soles of their shoes, the grandmother's smooth sneakers, the grandson's All-Star tread with squares and diagonals made more for basketball court than mountain trail. Among theirs the mark of the dog, a yellow mutt named after a character in an Earnest Thompson Seton tale— Lobo—a dog more latrans than lupus familiaris. In early August you might even see the occasional remnant of a raspberry drupelet, evidence that the boy was wrist-deep in the pail of picked raspberries, cramming them into a greedy mouth. You might even imagine the grandmother's admonishments for every berry eaten was one not jellied for winter toast.

Then again, you might think about what lay ahead on the path as it snaked through the brush and dropped off the bench. You might even listen a bit and hear over the call of meadowlark or the soft conversation of western bluebird the voice of the creek ahead.

As the way falls off the south slope, the temperature drops as it nears the creek, and the route picks up the shade of an occasional juniper, and lower, young aspen making a charge up the slope. Then you are there beside the stream in the cool shade of blue spruce reaching up and up to a bluer sky.

It is not much of a stream but raspberries grow thick on its banks for the grandmother and the stream bends and pools and forms dark holes perhaps two feet deep for the boy. Holes of mystery that work beneath the roots of towering spruce sometimes disappearing completely to come out the other side.

The boy and the grandmother spend entire afternoons here even when it is not berry season, Lobo lolling muddy in the shade, the boy belly down with his face inches from the water, the grandmother doing this and that, a notebook in her hand, sometimes flowers plucked from stem and folded into the pages of the notebook. At night, back in the ranch kitchen, atop the metal table, the flowers are carefully pressed between pieces of waxed paper and huge books—some the Latin and Greek textbooks of her long-past university education—weigh the flowers flat. When they are dried, the flowers are mounted on cardboard and framed as gifts for friends. Family. Captioned in the grandmother's perfect cursive: Rocky Mountain Columbine, Aquilegia coerulea, Shorty Creek, August 1971. Scarlet Gilia, Ipomopsis aggregata, Waugh Mountain, July 1972.

He cuts the bottom from a coffee can and stretches cellophane across the new mouth of it so he can telescope down into the water, watching the bugs crawl on the floor of the stream in its forest curve. He sees fish, tiny things, some with remanent egg sacks trailing from distended bellies and he imagines them trout although he has never seen a fish longer than the diameter of a dime. Sometimes the telescope leaks and he comes up with better designs using glue and rubber bands to hold the plastic window. But when that does not work and the coffee can still leaks, he just uses his eyes for the water is clear as air and the life crawls on the bottom and on the rocks and can be seen in the shade of the woods.

When the berries are in, he is enticed with promises of lemonade and such to pick a few, the first ones plinking into the tin pail, until the plink becomes a nearly inaudible soft plop and layers are added.

The grandmother works bent in sun and shade and rises occasionally to stretch a middle-aged kink and pulls a tissue from the fold of a sleeve, uses it, tucks it back for later use. She was a Great Depression mother of four and everything has a first use and then a second. Her pail fills before his and then she takes the boy's and fills that too while he wades in wet sneakers into cold water and thick mud. The shoes squish and squeak on the hike up the path toward the house and by the time the south-facing hot slope is navigated, they are only damp.

This is during the summers before the boy can drive. Years later, he arrives in his own car on a morning during berry season and he does not find the grandmother at the house but he sees her soft tread on the path to the creek and he follows. Ginna, he shouts, Ginna? She is known to all the grandchildren by this version of her first name—Virginia. When he finds her, she is sitting by the stream, right hand trailing in the water, sitting quiet and then he is there saying her name and she jerks up, startled. Her face blank, eyes too. Who? Then sweeps recognition, the circuits visibly firing, a smile breaking. Tommy! She laughs. Where were you Ginna? Underwater?

Many years later he visits her again, inside where she is safe from wandering, where the doors are locked from the outside and cannot be opened without a passkey. She looks off somewhere when he speaks her name and she does not look up in recognition but down at her hands where she sees, perhaps, an underwater world or a stream where raspberries grow wild under an endlessly, impossibly blue sky.

In the heart of the Gila

Under the fly, in that gray moment between dawn and dark, between sleep and consciousness, there is the rattle of rain. As it always does when you are laid out beneath nylon in the great outdoors, it sounds like more than it really is. Away from the amplification of drop on taut material, it is a light drizzle, but in this moment of sort-of-awake, sort-of-not, the ears say it is a downpour. And there are few things more soul-soothing than lying half-awake listening to rain patter on your tent while you are warm and dry.

The auditory: A sparrow tittering off somewhere in the ponderosas on the ridge above. The sound of the river. Gathering light. Robins now and a nuthatch somewhere out there, head-first on a pine trunk, walking straight down as if there is no such thing as gravity or height, foraging, moving, a cease-less babble as he goes, like a child on an Easter egg hunt. One of the horses paws and snorts on the highline out there and now I come awake and aware. The pines. The birds. The light shower. The river. The Gila.

Coffee. Need coffee.

As Abbey's Hayduke chanted, "chemicals, chemicals, must have chemicals," I light the stove and wait that impatient wait for river-water to boil and for that first sip of coffee. That first sip. An enchanting moment, like the first sip of an ice-cold beer after a sweat-hard day of building fence under angry sun. Sudden. Refreshing. Magical. Like the first time you lay eyes on new country.

This is our new country and one that we have been living with for days now, three humans, one lean bird dog and eight good rough-country horses. This is our first taste of the Gila. On day one, we slack-jawed at big daddy bull pines with trunks greater in diameter than a football huddle. We rode up the Middle Fork beneath cliffs that reiterated the insignificance of mankind, passing through life zones as one might stroll casually through city neighborhoods. Here a ponderosa, there a juniper with a hide like an alligator's (and named such), there an Arizona sycamore with leaves as large as an infant's head. Boxelder and oak and, suddenly, oddly, a Douglas fir. And now, of all things, a spruce. A spruce three thousand miles away from boreal forest.

We are here for a fish. A trout named Gila. Named after the country or perhaps a chicken-egg thing. The trout then the country? Or the country then the trout? La Trucha de Gila. Upstream from our camp a baker's dozen miles is another camp with a big meadow and a herd of three dozen mules. There, in an expedition that would put General Crook's Apache campaign in perspective, are men and women on Gila trout duty, surveying the West Fork and a few obscure tributaries for remnant populations of what many consider the West's rarest cold-water piscus.

It is human trait to collect, to gather. In some, it is an illness that manifests itself in mounds of cat crap and twin-headed feline inbreds. But in others it is a more modest affliction.

I am a collector of game and fish. It was O'Connor and his "grand slam" who made me pine for a hunt of each of the four wild sheep on this continent, a grail that I have filled only one-quarter of the way in a lifetime. I have taken each of the half dozen species of quail in this country over the points of many generations of good setters. I have chased after members of the deer family from Alaska to Arizona.

Then there's the native trout. Rio Grandes and the greenbacks of my youth, Apache trout in college days between keggers, the northern cutthroats, and then a tiny redband from a larch forest stream. But the Gila, never the Gila, a fish as tan as a buckskin gelding, a fish of the desert, a trout as rare as a cool breeze on a Phoenix summer day.

It was not until the 1950s that we recognized the Gila as a species, a cold-water loving trout swimming in the mountains of southern New Mexico just a skip from the border of Old Mexico. By then it was almost too late, for that fish we all love to hate (and love), the rainbow, had found its way into the Gila Mountains. Rainbows love their cross-pollination and the Gila trout was no exception. For thousands of years, it had toughed it out in tepid waters, survived drought, fire, flood. But in only a sprinkle of a few decades, it was nearly gone, hybridized, gene-pool pollution almost everywhere. Pure, native Gila were found in a half dozen tiny streams in the toughest, highest, meanest holds of the range. These were streams that barely held water, that during the dry season dwindled to puddle and trickle. By 1967, the Gila ended up on "The List" and being on it meant no fishing and likely extinction. But things very slowly began to turn, barge-like. Forty years later, in 2006, the trout was downgraded to "threatened" status and a few places were opened to limited sport fishing thanks to big-time recovery efforts on the part of state and federal fisheries biologists. Men and women like Jim Brooks—a Gila trout enthusiast, mule-packer extraordinaire, and fisheries biologist with stints in federal and state agencies—and Jill Wick—a quiet New Mexico fisheries biologist whose smile when holding a Gila from a native stream says it all. These two and others who have made the Gila trout recovery a career, but also a passion, are shaped by the country, inspired by the trout. People with a zeal for the rare air that is a cold-water fish in an increasingly warm world. For anglers like me and my friends, that means we will be able to attempt to catch one of the rarest fish in the world because of their commitment and work.

For as long as I have been able to read, the Gila—the land, not the trout—has been on my "bucket list." Terry Tempest Williams wrote an essay in which she recounts being able to remember the exact place and time she first read Aldo Leopold's A Sand County Almanac. So can I. I was a teenager on the porch of my grandmother's ranch house in southeastern Colorado. Though a man of Iowa and Wisconsin for some, Aldo for me will always mean the Gila, a landscape that he used, along with his saddle horse Polly, to define the concept of wilderness.

Leopold wrote that wilderness needed to be big enough to absorb a two-weeks' horseback trip, requiring a big piece of country of hundreds of thousands of acres, not the comparatively tiny acreages being proposed today. In 1924, thanks to Polly and Aldo, the Gila became our country's first bona fide wilderness area, a swath of ponderosa and yucca, chasm and park, of nearly three-quarters of a million acres. Forty years before the wilderness act of 1964. The Gila is a legend on a plane with the The Bob in Montana and The Frank in Idaho. A landscape far bigger than its reputation. Which is saying something.

We have come to this camp where the coffee is now hot in the mug and the rain has slacked, to experience the fish, certainly. But also to experience the land. Rugged and tough and sometimes downright scary, but as Leopold wrote, "it must be poor life that achieves freedom from fear." A few days ago, my gelding Red refused to continue down a particularly snarled section of trail. Not like big Red. But then I stopped cussing him and listened and there in the trail, coiled in menace, was a rattlesnake chilling my core with his buzz. We made camp that night in a beautiful bench of stirrup-high grass and I thanked Red for his mountain savvy. The following morning, we rode up a thin path into the woods, climbing sharply from the river bottom. The trail narrowed, dwindled, caved away. Rocks and deadfall everywhere. Suddenly, two of the pack horses tripped, slipped, and fell, plunging and tumbling down off the trail, rolling ears over ass again and again to the valley floor. Nature was not twittering birds and gentle rain, instead it was rockfall and panic in a wild tumble of equine and human alike. Unbelievably, the horses stood up at the bottom and started grazing, unhurt. Trying to calm our pounding hearts, we regrouped, repacked and scrambled up over a route that had seen neither boot- nor hoof-print all season. We have not seen any faces other than our own for days.

This is mesa and canyon country. Pines and junipers on the tops and slopes, cottonwoods and tangle in the stream bottoms. The canyons, ridges and streams speak to us of heritage and story lost: Bloodgood, Rawmeat, Wild Cow. Descriptive too: Brushy, Rough, Cave, Spring. And still other names that make you wonder who: Nat Straw and Tom Moore canyons. The saddles in this country are not just leather, but passes through tough country: Hummingbird Saddle, No Name, Turkeyfeather.

Epic wildfires came a half-decade ago, fires of a scale that had never been seen before. Whole drainages fried to a char beyond anything Dante could dream up. Gila trout were trucked out of rough country in buckets on pack mules or slung beneath helicopters. Streams boiled. Fish died.

In some ways, it was a tragedy beyond words. But in other ways, for the Gila trout, it was a sudden, if unusual, boon. Fire does not discriminate. It kills rainbow trout as easily as Gila. Entire stream systems now had not one trout. A million gallons of rotenone and an army of fisheries biologists could not accomplish what the wildfires did in a matter of hours. And the fires burned right through all of that red tape that would have had to accompany a similar mission of the bureaucracy. Now, for the first time in generations, some drainages in the Gila are free of invasive species like browns and rainbows. Slowly, carefully, and expensively, Gila are being replanted into these streams. Here, in the desert, they are far more adept than their rainbow cousins from the great Northwest. These are streams that drizzle down to garden hose strength, to pools that get as warm as back porch sun tea. No place for a fish from the glaciers of Washington.

Upstream from our camp, the fisheries biologists smile as they find pure, genuine native trout in streams that were repopulated a few years ago. Zero rainbow genes.

Before us is our stream, the stream we drink in our coffee, the stream I will fish today, fly rod in hand, hope in my heart. I will take to the water as a prospector might with an eager pan, hoping for a few flakes of gold, hoping to touch something precious. This rare experience is not taking place on a Russian peninsula or a turquoise reef off the coast of Africa. It is taking place right here in this country just a hair north of the border.

La Trucha de Gila.

Time

This day—this bright, clear, unbelievably sharp mountain meadow day—has me thinking of time. We walk outside the willow wall that hugs the creek's meander. Up on the bench above the stream among elk thistle and cinquefoil, fly rods in hand. It is day one.

We do this every year. Not this place. New places when we can. Old places too. The point is not so much the place as it is the rendezvous. We don't see each other often, for we are busy men with a shared passion for the outdoors, trout, open country, life, our work. Three friends who happen to work together and yet can set it aside to join for a few rare days of just fishing. I caution my pals to live in the moment. This moment. It is day one. Soon it will be day two and then it will be over. Days go like that. Years too. Decades.

So, the stream. It is a bending number, doubling back on itself. One can drop into a bend, walk into the creek's coolness, work upstream for an hour screened by willow jungle from the road and the pickup, and then peek out to find he has only traveled one hundred yards or so from the parking lot. Or, as we are doing now, one can walk on the bench and make some time. Most people, near as we can tell from the tracks, start fishing at the parking lot, so the far water is where we head.

We take turns. In the deep pools, we spot fish. Sometimes, we look at the water and it is blank, even though we are cautious and quiet in our approach. Other times, a polarized peer discovers a half dozen good-sized fish moving and feeding.

I am up first. So I cast to the head of a small run where the visible music that is current coming together from all angles forms a liquid line, a feeding lane. Mend just right and the fly drifts well, looking good. There's a rise and the fish is on, putting a good kink in the light rod. I can't tell what kind of fish it is until it comes within two feet of my outstretched hand in the clear water. Then I see blue and purple and iridescence brighter than that wonderful sea of blue yonder above. A big fin. A sail fin. I think of flying fish on a brilliant ocean and then the fish is in my hand. Grayling. I have caught something as rare as a comet in the night sky. A survivor. He and his kind have lasted ten or even twelve thousand years, left here by ice melt and glacial dam. Now living in a mountain stream in a high country valley alongside modern man. He has seen our kind traveling by foot, on horseback, Model A and Audi and yet still here he is. We have gone from wearing animal skins tanned with brain, to poly-blend shirts with pockets everywhere and built in sun-protection. Yet still here he is. Still in this stream despite the odds. A special fish.

He has a wound in his side, perhaps a heron stab, or a miscalculation when swimming among the sharp willow of a beaver dam, but he is vigorous and healthy. A tail flips and he is back in the water. Next man is up. We look for more fish, walking slowly, pushing through willows, slapping bugs, thinking of pissed-off moose mothers and maybe even a bear in the cool shade, but mostly just there, spotting fish, helping each other.

Another grayling rises to a well-placed fly and we admire and take pictures and then carefully release and the next man steps into the pool and catches his own bit of treasure. The hour passes as hours do, and then the sun leans back a bit and we light cigars and sit on the bank and watch clouds and their shadows on the mountain.

In this moment on the bank, on this annual assemble, we have each touched a precious living diamond. A fish from time. A survivor. This moment in time will be enough to hold us for another year. For the next time.

Fishing with Otto

The pond is two miles away by bicycle and it consumes our days. Even when we are not there, we scheme. A friend wades with me into its tepid darkness and we stretch an old bedsheet between us. This homemade seine net is plunged and scraped across the pond's muddy bottom and then up onto the shore where treasures—mudpuppies and crayfish and fathead minnows—thrash violently to return in the wild scramble to put them in jars and coffee cans. Then we wobble our bikes home, water slopping, innocent creatures trapped and doomed despite a new plastic wading pool with clean water. The creatures all perish, and their sad carcasses go into writhing ant piles.

There is an undaunted pond on return.

These are the things that consume the nine-year-old soul in the spring and summer of 1970. Worms go on hooks and into streams and sometimes trout are caught. Brook trout mostly, once in a great while a brown or even a rainbow. They swim in water as clear as air and there is crawling and peering into that water, the world small and in control. There is no time for looking up, forward, beyond. I do not think about anything but the now, the world at my feet. I do not think about needs other than present or family other than immediate. I do not think about skylines or futures or old men, even old men named Grandpa.

But now, in this moment, Grandpa is here. Decades gone and he arrives daily. Grandpa Otto would have known how to do this, be a father, a provider, a rock. He would have known how to deal with the worry, even the fear that seems to hang in the air like the sickness. Worry for others and for what we have built and the fear of losing everything. He would have known. I call his son, my father, and ask but he was a young boy in that Greatest of Depressions, looking at that world through nine-year-old eyes, his world in his grasp and no cares.

Otto lived it but he is not here to ask. The lament of the living is in the not-asking, the too-late-now. His life: the end of horses, a pandemic and a world war, a boom, a ruined economy, another world war and a recovery. This grandfather who always seemed old, I want to ask him about this world, the sickness, the anger, the fear, the wreckage to the economy caused by the virus.

His math is easy, multiples of ten. He was ten at the crack of a new century, twenty when there were only a half million cars spread between 92 million people. Twenty-eight for the sickness that pulled the breath from 675,000 out of a population of 103 million. Forty when he entered the decade that put one in four out of work, 55 when the war ended and he could stop driving 65 miles one way in a 1936 Chevrolet burning half rationed gasoline and half kerosene to spend a week sleeping in a boarding house and days in a factory making machine gun bullets. An old man of 80 when I am a boy looking up.

Now, in the very beginning of our own pandemic, our own promise of a ruined economy, I think about old men, about my kind, gentle 90-year-old father who bent to work just as Otto did. I worry about him and my 86-year-old mother, sequestered in their mountain home where a nine-year-old once lived with mudpuppies and hapless crayfish. A father brittle as homestead windowpane with emphysema and a walker and a mother still cooking for him every day because that is what she did and does and that is their way. Stay away from people, I say, but they do and did before all of this happened. They have been social distancing for 20 years. All they have is each other because their friends are gone either to warmer climates or heavenly ones. Their state is much more populous, thus perilous, than my family's but this does not help with the worry in these early weeks, the news filled with a cloud of concern, businesses shut down, scenes of refrigerated trucks outside hospitals where bodies stack like cordwood. It is early and we just don't know. Not knowing is the thing.

In the early days of the pandemic, a fishing pal calls about hitting the Jefferson early this year and the conversation swings into flippant territory, the glib ignorance of rural white America. I don't think this is going to amount to much, he says.

Yeah, hell, what is it now, like 130 for the whole country? I ask. More people died on Montana highways this year and it's only March.

This is a part of a conversation, mostly about fly fishing, that will be rewound and replayed. Where the passion arose is unknown. Magazines, perhaps. A little bit from an uncle who dabbled in fly tying and once pinned a gold ribbed hare's ear, fresh from the vise, to a boy's cap.

It came from water, certainly, but fly-casting was self-taught from reading McClane, Wulff, others. Stood on the lawn and practiced. One wise author determined that the best way to tell a reader, the budding fly fisherman, not to tie wind knots was to write about how to tie wind knots. This is a habit it will take 20 years to break. But still I stand there on the lawn and cast while the pond buddies get caught up in ball sports. My sport is fishing, a fever whose origin is untraceable. It did not come from Otto, who never once fished in any memory. Who is to say how many sparks are needed on the tinder? Perhaps there need only be one.

The fishing trips with Otto's son, however, are each as sharp in memory as dawn sunlight after night rain. There is a September drive in the 1979 Ford halfton that the old man still owns up out of Colorado and into Wyoming where the clean cold waters of the Green come from the stone knuckles of a mountain range named after a weather feature: Wind.

Otto had been dead only a few years then, and now looking back over long years and short ones too, I wonder if my father thought about his own while fishing with his son. That trip is as clean in memory as if it were a year ago instead of more than 30. Perhaps this is a function of rarity, as one might remember with absolute brilliance a whispering glimpse of a wild wolf or grizzly in the tall timber. The fishing trips with my father were not many, but clarity of rarity trumps quantity any day.

My father's math is easy too. Three. Three. Thirty. He's ninety. I should have been there for that landmark birthday, but had other things to do, a common lament and lament too strong a word. It is an excuse that is so worn it feels as familiar as old flannel. Call on his birthday and he makes jokes about his age as he has for 20 years and your mother gets on the other line and they talk over one another and say what? a lot in a routine that could double as a comedy skit. They talk to each other on the phones as much as they talk to their son. What did he say? I can't hear him, can you Chuck? Oh, oh, yes, we are driving over to get the groceries and they come out and put them in the trunk and we don't even have to say anything. The pandemic takes care of any niggling thoughts of visits, provides the full-blown excuse. When the World Health Organization officially names it a global pandemic, our calls are more frequent. It is real now and there are signs everywhere. The signs out on the Interstate used to flash drunk driving warnings, highway death tolls. Now they flash messages about staying home, staying away from people, this new social distancing phrase that becomes forever the world's lexicon.

There are so many questions. I do not want to be unable to ask, to wish for just one more question. I call often now, and chuckle through the comedy skit and ask them both about their parents, growing up in a Great Depression when Otto made a dollar a day cutting timber alongside the Big Thompson, a famous trout river that he never fished. About both of them growing up in the shadow of a 14,000-foot peak. Work. Work. Always work. Fishing was for food, belly-crawling beneath that tall peak to little streams where brook trout slammed up out of the shadows because a dollar a day cannot buy much supper for four appetites and a boy with a fishing rod can do his part.

Otto was 40 when my father was born and it was 1930 and now there were two children to feed and the world going to hell for a dollar a day. I am 56 when Otto is born. He is my first and only child. A son. Coming back from another fly-fishing trip I learned I was having a son after a week spent catching golden trout and mackinaw beneath a mountain named after a weather feature: Cloud. I pull over on the side of the road in the hot desert and shout. A son.

The idea of Otto did not come easily and did not come with great style. Otto's mother is more than two decades younger. My vision for a life then did not include a child, was never one that appealed. Bamboo rods hand-made over in Twin Bridges, Winchester Model 70s, combination caribou-Arctic char adventures on the Itkillik. That appeals. A squalling infant? Not only no, but hell no. The relationship does not last long.

But neither does the breakup, or the next reunion or the next breakup. She is a quiet stunningly beautiful woman, still waters, with deep brown eyes and long brown hair and on the Big Hole one spring I know I am done for. She is in the bow of the drift boat, casting long, tight loops. She casts better than I ever will despite all the lawn practice, the Wulff and the McClane, the hacking away for more than 40 years. Pass a drift boat of three men. They are working an eddy to rising fish in the upcurrent and they all stop, look away from the rising fish, and stare. The fish keep rising and the oarsman quits rowing and they all stare.

After returning from the South Fork and another fishing trip, I write her a long letter and tell her that the mind and the heart are changed. Truly changed. There will be no going back and I find that I want it and maybe wanted it for longer than I admit.

Otto is born on Winter Solstice, a harbinger of longer days and spring a long way off but coming. Two years later, pre-pandemic, he and his sister climb into the pickup and the three of us head 50 miles to a museum in the city. Mom needs a break. The museum has dinosaurs and a living reptile exhibit and the family minus Mom spends a lot of time peering through glass at the snakes, but eventually lands in the Yellowstone exhibit where a faux fishing pond for the kids includes a fishing pole with a magnet for a lure tossed into the "water" for "trout" which also have magnets in their noses. Otto stands on the bridge over the "water" catching "trout" for an hour and when he is picked up to leave, he squalls loud enough for other parents to stop what they are doing and glance a knowing look that says, "Poor man." But Otto's passion brings a smile and a hope to the heart.

In the early days, before Otto could crawl, there is math. Sixty-five, maybe retired, Otto nine. Seventy-four, he is 18. Eighty and 24. There are no more afternoon beers or summer cigars and they are not missed. Much. The bird dogs and the mind are exercised. I want quantity and clarity for my son, for his memories. Now there is other math. The day the governor announces the pending "stay at home" order there are 1,296 dead in this big nation. Two days later when it goes into effect, there are 2,222. I call the parents again and they fumble through technology that will allow them to see their grand-child, their only grandchild, online. Mostly there is a good look at their kitchen ceiling.

Daycare closed. School closed. The neighbor has a real pond and says go ahead. We walk down there through the east horse pasture, climb a fence, Otto on the shoulders, his sister riding her white and pink bike through the wheatgrass. Hand the fly rod to Otto and the spin rod to his sister. She catches a fish and Otto thrashes the water with the fly rod. There is no hook anyway. He throws the rod down, a cheap pawn shop special, and starts throwing sticks and pretending he is fishing. Twenty minutes go by and the sister is done. When you pick up Otto to leave, he scares geese off the field next to the pond with hollering and tears. "I go fishing. I go fishing."

The pond lies between the post office and home and every time you pass the neighbor's place in the days after, from the backseat, "Dada I go fishing. Dada I go fishing."

Mud season in Montana and the days trail on. Snow, cold, wind, sun, rain, repeat. Attempting to be a good parent, partner, employee, son. The virus is an old people killer and there is a sharp fear for them. Some days it is just the old parents and the questions on the phone. Both are asked to write a letter to their grandchild so he will know. There are a lot of questions, miles of air between Montana and Colorado and being reminded of what good people they are, how generous, the life they gave of adventure and mudpuppies in farm ponds. How was that forgotten and why did it take a global crisis? How is it that life takes one up into its vortex and spins the soul around and years with it?

The virus kills jobs too. Millions. One in seven out of work. My father recounts a story of unlacing Otto's tall logging boots before the warmth of the coal stove because Otto was too tired after a day on the timber crew to do it himself. He talks about Otto's big promotion when he supervised the crew and went to a dollar and a quarter a day, a raise that put other food on the table alongside the freshcaught brook trout. The juggling of a good stay-home office job and young children at home all day long seems trivial when measured by this tape. The neighbor's pond is visited several times and Otto reels in his first fish, a brook trout, shouting, "Mine, mine, mine!" Why do they always shout?

Two weeks into the new routine of teaching and parenting and employment, a day is needed for solo adult time. Each adult gets a day a week. On my day, the pickup is packed with two bird dogs, a lawn chair, a cooler, beer, a fly rod. It is still early for high country adventures and snow blocks the road to the cutthroat in the river up-valley, so the pickup is steered up a dirt road that has always beckoned. The two-track leads to a tributary out in the sagebrush.

I drive slowly, crawling in four-low, cautious on a road that has just thawed clear of the winter's blanket. Out onto a sagebrush bench and the stream small enough to hop across and a meadow of winter-mashed old grass. Park. The dogs burst out into the day, to their running and sniffing. I sit there in the good warmth of early April, jacket warmth, but warmth nevertheless. I think about a people who never knew leisure and the next generation who knew just a little bit of it and put themselves through college, and a next generation who had the outdoors as luxury instead of hurdle and college tuition paid. Listen to the discrete conversations of mountain bluebirds up out of Central America, prospecting the brown-going-green of early spring in Montana and smile as the dogs go bursting past. Mostly I think about the family and all of that noise and a sudden aching loneliness without it.

When cell service was left this morning, there were 12,000 American victims of COVID-19. When I am back in range and the news feed checked, there are 14,600.

Later in the day, the lawn chair folded and packed, the bird dogs tired, muddy and pulling rosebush twigs from their fur in the back seat, the pickup tires hit pavement along the main river. Downstream, below the dam, is a fishing access that on early season weekdays should be vacant, but there are four pickups there. Others are seeking pandemic relief. I stop anyway, string up Otto's pawn shop special, put on a real fly, leave the dogs in the pickup with the windows down.

In the thick alder and willow, I scramble on a fishing trail that has been used by fellow COVID escapees, moose, deer, cattle. Eventually I find the river and a deep, folding-back eddy that holds trout. Swing a soft hackle through it, once, twice and then feel the tap-tap, and lift the rod tip into it. It is a good fish and it flashes in the water until it tires and I touch its sleekness in the water. I think for a minute holding it gently in the water, think for a minute longer, pull the fish out, flip it upside down and give one sharp decisive tap on a big rock. It has been years, decades even, since I killed a trout, but I kneel there and clean it and remember how my father taught this lesson, where to cut, how to thumb the bloodline. Think about how good it will be to feed the family this fish, a tiny provision, but providing all the same. Then I start back up the path to the truck and home, looking forward and up, knowing somehow that no matter what is ahead there is always a way and we will endure if we find it.

Why Do I Like This Sport?

The rain put the mosquitoes down. It came slowly at first, pushing up in the pines, spattering against the tarp. It always sounds as if it is raining harder than it really is when you are lying under a tarp or a tent. I kept my head down in my sleeping bag, not because of the rain that blew in sometimes from the side and onto my bed, but because of the bugs. They had been whining all night and I sweated hot in my sleeping bag and cursed them and cursed forgetting to bring a headnet and a tent instead of a nylon fly. I had wanted to go minimalist but the mosquitoes brought hard regret to that scenario.

It was too late, too far in, too much literal blood spilled to turn back. The mountains are named the Pioneers and I can only think of that pioneering spirit, somehow taking resolve in men and women long dead who didn't have the luxury of bug dope, nylon tarps and down sleeping bags.

But the rain put the bugs down, especially when it came harder and with lightning that danced on the ridges above my little river valley, that flashed and struck and boomed and trembled the earth quicker than you can read these words. I hunkered down and listened to it coming hard, wind up loud, lightning dancing. I thought about my fly rod leaning up against a tree and remembered something about reading that lightning was attracted to graphite. The mosquitoes an afterthought now. But the storm moves, rolls across the mountains and I hear it booming loud, then softer, then a distant flash and rumble down off over the valley where the lights of Dillon crease the very thin edge of the eastern sky.

Breakfast comes and the bugs with it, almost immediately. It is as if they are born right there in the rain-washed grass and for all I know, they are. I swat them frantically, then tell myself to calm down, superstitious that bugs are attracted to thrashing like sharks to wounded bait fish. I pour a pile of yellow garlic powder into my hashbrowns, thinking maybe that will work.

The stream is out beyond camp, behind the willows. Last night, I had time for a few casts, and caught a few thick, fat cutthroats in the bended water of the meanders. Enough to laugh a bit and enough to distract me for a few seconds from the blood fest going on around my head and on my arms and bare legs. I laid on the bug dope then, and am not out of the hot sweaty sleeping bag a minute before I slather on more. My more crunchy friends would chastise me for the chemical repellent and urge me toward citronella or something. But there is a frenzy going on and I coat on the DEET. Give me chemicals! I'll take my chances.

The bugs drive me to the stream. In places, the deepest bends, I can get my bare legs down into the water to just above the knee. At least the bugs can't get me underwater, so I slash through the willow, ignoring the itch of nettle on my calves, and submerge. The water feels good on old bites from last night.

I am in a slick run that bends through willow. There are mink and elk tracks on the sandbar at the head of the pool, and debris—pine needles and old aspen leaves and gray-dead corpses of willow and alder—piled up above the water line. The water at the head of the pool forms an edge and I make a slow, easy cast and ease the fly onto the water. A fish rises quickly, a slashing splash, and I miss the hook set and the fly is behind me, trapped on a tall willow, wound around it and not coming off. I slap at mosquitoes and tell myself, for the thousandth time, to keep a calm demeanor, and reach high into the willow where my fly is pinned. It is out of my reach, so I pull down hard on the willow and the branch snaps out of my grasp, tightening suddenly on my line and snapping back and the tippet gives. There is the fly, up in the damned tree. I can see it. But the bugs are eating me alive, feasting on my white legs. I dive back in the water and the bugs come with me, whining like 10,000 tiny helicopters in my ears. I dig through my fly box and bugs coat the backs of my hands, impervious to a fresh coat of DEET. Or maybe I somehow washed it off.

I tie on another fly now. Swatting.

It is like this for an hour or more—the rhythm and beauty of fly fishing something so distant I think I may have read about it when I was a kid once. On this stream of fly-trapping willow and insect predators, it seems like a myth. Why do I like this sport?

I find a nice pool, make a cast and the fly wraps twice around the overhanging fingers of a willow at the head of the pool. I pull at the snag and the fly snaps back into my face and snags in my shirt collar. I spend what seems like ten minutes trying to unhook the fly, getting eaten alive. Now there are horse flies and those bastards hurt. The only good thing about them is I can feel them bite my flesh and they are slow carnivores and usually die with a hard slap before they can fly away with a chunk of my meat in their jaws. Ugly creatures with psychedelic tie-dye eyes and they squish satisfactorily to my yelp and slap dance. Sonofabitch! Slap!

Why do I like this sport?

The sun is up and hot-full now and the mosquitoes are down somewhat. The horse flies, though, take over this shift. That and the deer flies, triangular black bodies, quicker than the big flies, and just as painful. One of my hands is swelling slightly from bites, a minor allergic reaction I've gotten used to.

I work up the stream, casting and slapping and not much catching. Small cutts rise eagerly for my dry fly, but there is no joy in the day. Once, I slip on a submerged dead alder lying coppery and slick beneath the surface, and go down. I land face down, catching myself with my left, raising the rod high in my right, protecting it. At the last second I drop the rod so it won't snap as I go down. I am wet to the chest, but it oddly feels good. Some of the bugs have bitten through my shirt and the wet cotton is a relief. I pull the rod out of the water, and wash the reel free from sand and grit, and blow on it and then wash it again. It is a while before the grating of sand on metal disappears when I turn the handle.

I make the beaver ponds, still awkward, not going right. It hasn't gone right since I left the truck at the trailhead, I don't think. Some trips are just like that. Not right. Stumbling. Stubborn. Going on.

I work up to the top of the pond and make a few casts that land okay. Land well, in fact, and I catch a few cutthroat now that are bigger. I move to the next pond where it pushes up against a sage-cloaked hillside and decide to climb. Maybe the bugs will be okay up there on the sagebrush and at least I can look down into the pond and see if there are any fish worth it.

In wet felt-bottom sandals, I slip on the grass, and go down again, thrusting out my left hand and drawing blood on sharp gravel. Why do I like this sport? I grab handfuls of sagebrush, whole stems of it, and climb higher, up to a small rock pile and I lean out over the pond and look down.

It lies out slick before me, this pond. Shallow at the dam and mud like wet dust loose at the base. Thick, bottomless muck. Deeper near the head, with channels for the dam-builders. A drowned willow mid-pond. I see a few fish, swimming lazily. Foot-long trout. None are rising. But at the head of the pool, I see a shape. I look for a long time before I realize I am looking at a tail. The tail of a really big trout. A trout of perhaps two feet. I watch him now and he rises slowly and takes a drowned ant off the surface, then slowly down. I see the white as his mouth opens, then closes, then he goes back to his soft finning in thick clear water. I feel an excitement rising, almost as if the little blood left in my body from the attack of the killer insects is coming back up in my arms and chest. I have ant patterns in my fly box.

This is why.

About the Author

A life-long man of the American West, author Thomas
Reed grew up fishing small streams from the ponderosa pine-clad
mountains of Arizona to the lodgepole pine forests of Montana and
many places in between. He is the author of several books and has
been a long-time columnist for *Wyoming Wildlife* magazine, where his
popular "Wild Country Dispatch" column has appeared for many
years, and the quarterly magazine *TROUT*, which features his "Blue
Lines" column in every issue. *Blue Lines, A Fishing Life* is his story and
shows us fishing as a healer, fishing as common ground between ad-
versaries, and fishing as a way to connect families through the generations. He lives with his family on a ranch outside Pony, Montana.